Key Stage 3

Maths

Ages 13–14

Sheila Hunt

survival GUIDE

Letts Educational
Chiswick Centre
414 Chiswick High Road
London W4 5TF
Tel: 020 8996 3333
Fax: 020 8742 8390
Email: mail@lettsed.co.uk
Website: www.letts-education.com

First published 2001
Reprinted 2002

British Library Cataloging in Publication Data. A CIP record of this book is available from the British Library.

ISBN 1 84085 638 6

Letts Educational Limited is a division of Granada Learning Limited, part of the Granada Media Group.

Edited and typeset by Cambridge Publishing Management

Designed by Moondisks Limited

Maths

Book 3 Ages 13-14

Introduction

Decisions, decisions! Year 9 is a year of decisions. Are you going to take geography or art? What about P.E. or drama? Which sets will you be in? This book can't make the choices for you, but it may help you to make the decisions that are right for you. Many of you will be taking the Key Stage 3 National Tests, or SATs as you probably call them. These are divided into levels, and your maths tests will probably cover Levels 4–6, 5–7 or 6–8.

Inside *Letts Key Stage 3 Maths Survival Guide Ages 13–14*, you'll find enough maths to cover anything which you may find on SATS papers, up to and including Level 7, and checklists towards the back of the book with details of the topics that you need to know from Levels 5 to 8. Also, to give you some idea of what to expect in the SATs, there are specimen questions for you to try, clearly marked with the required level.

There are handy tips too in the 'Survival Sheets' to help you plan your time, and also to give you some pointers to help you make those all important decisions.

The number network

If you used the Ages 11–12 or Ages 12–13 books from this series, you may recognise the number network. The Ages 13–14 version has a few extra connections to guide you through the coming year. If you haven't seen the number network before, don't panic. It's for reference only, and you are not expected to learn it! The number network is a quick way to check up on the skills you need before you tackle a new topic or process. You can't, for example, solve circle questions without some knowledge of area and perimeter. The number network shows you which areas you need to know before you tackle something new, and also just how far that newly-acquired skill could take you.

Have a good trip!

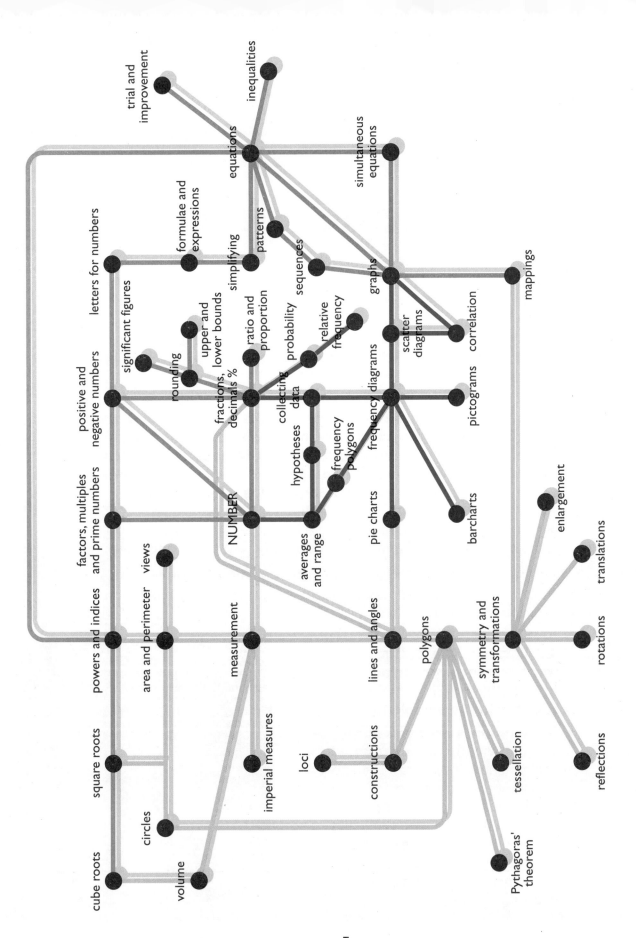

trial and improvement

inequalities

equations

simultaneous equations

formulae and expressions

simplifying

patterns

sequences

graphs

mappings

letters for numbers

significant figures

upper and lower bounds

ratio and proportion

probability

relative frequency

scatter diagrams

correlation

rounding

fractions, decimals %

collecting data

frequency diagrams

pictograms

positive and negative numbers

hypotheses

frequency polygons

factors, multiples and prime numbers

NUMBER

averages and range

pie charts

barcharts

enlargement

views

translations

powers and indices

area and perimeter

measurement

lines and angles

polygons

symmetry and transformations

rotations

square roots

imperial measures

loci

constructions

tessellation

reflections

circles

Pythagoras' theorem

cube roots

volume

1

How to tackle questions

Have you ever read through a maths question and found yourself asking, 'What do they want me to do?'? If only you could tell what the question was asking, you might be able to answer it quite easily, but as it is ... no chance! Many of us have been there at some stage, so don't despair. Help is at hand. With time and practice, it will probably dawn on you that some words and situations keep cropping up.

- Questions on Pythagoras' theorem always involve right-angled triangles. If you were setting a question on Pythagoras' theorem, you would have to find a situation where a right angle occurs somewhere – hence all those ladders against a wall, towers, flagpoles. Of course, you will have to read the question carefully and not jump to conclusions. Right-angled triangles could also crop up in questions about angles, area or volume.

- As you read through a question, underline what the question is asking. Often this will be summarised in just a few words at the end. Knowing what you are eventually looking for can often start you off in the right direction.

- As you work, tick the information in the question as you use it. If you get stuck part way through, look back to the question – you may have overlooked a vital piece of information.

- Ask yourself, 'Why did they tell me that?' You usually need all the information provided in the question to find the solution.

- If a question is in several parts, you may need to use an answer that you have reached in one part to complete a later part. Remember, too, that even if you can't 'derive' or 'show that...' the answer in an early part of the question, you can still use it in the later parts and pick up a few extra marks.

- It is very useful if you know how marks are awarded for the question. If a question is only worth one mark, it must involve something fairly basic, such as the sum of the angles of a triangle. If three or more marks are available, then the answer is more complicated and requires some working out, which you should always write down. This means you may get some credit even if you don't reach the final correct answer.

- The same words and shapes keep cropping up in questions. To 'evaluate' means to find the value of something, and is very common in algebra questions. Be careful, too, to do what the question wants. If it asks you to draw, then you make an accurate drawing. If it asks you to sketch, you do not even have to use a ruler, provided that the diagram is a reasonable representation, and you have labelled everything that was given in the information.

- Be careful to distinguish between 'draw', 'construct or measure' and 'calculate'. To 'calculate' means to work out from the information given, so any diagram provided will neither be drawn accurately nor be to scale. You should not answer the question by an accurate drawing or by using measurements from the original question, although it is often helpful to provide a sketch to make clear what you are doing.

- Any reasons you supply to support your answer must be mathematically correct. 'It looks like a right angle' is not a mathematical reason and you may have jumped to a wrong conclusion if you are using a diagram that you have been told is inaccurate.

- The same topics often go together. A diagram of a shape with the angles marked may lead to a question involving angles and parallel lines. If you remember this from previous experience, it can help you to decide what the question is all about, but be prepared to change tactics if necessary.

- On shape questions, try filling in all the additional information that the question gives you without actually stating it. For example, if you have an angle marked on a straight line, then you can subtract that number from 180° and you have the value of any other angle or angles coming from the same point along the same straight line. Gather all the information that you can before you start to tackle the question and you may find that you have the problem licked before you start.

- Often you will be asked to 'give a reason for your answer'. If you can do this in symbols – particularly in an algebra question – you should do so, as it is good practice for answering GCSE questions, but only do this if you are absolutely sure that you are using the symbols properly. If you have any doubt, write the explanation in words. At this stage it is only important to show your teacher that you have worked the problem out correctly.

Rounding

Decimal places (d.p.)

Each digit after the decimal point is in a 'decimal place'. Count the digits after the decimal point.

0.8 has one place of decimals. It is correct to 1 d.p.

0.08 has two decimal places. It is correct to 2 d.p.

3.08 is also correct to 2 d.p.

Rounding – a reminder

Find the digit in the decimal place immediately after the number of decimal places you need. If its value is 4 or less, round down. If its value is 5 or more, round up.

> ### Example
> 3.9754 to 3 d.p. is 3.975   (4 or less, round down.)
>   to 2 d.p. is 3.98   (5 or more, round up.)
>   to 1 d.p. is 4.0   (You **must** have a digit to represent each decimal place specified.)

Significant figures (s.f. or sig. figs.)

Whether you are rounding a whole number, or one that includes decimal fractions, start with the first non-zero digit from the left.

A zero sandwiched between two non-zero digits is significant.

The rules about rounding up or down are the same as before.

0.8 has 1 s.f.

0.08 also has 1 s.f.

3.08 has 3 s.f.

Exercise 1

1 Give the following numbers correct to 1 d.p.
   a 0.86   **b** 4.338   **c** 0.45
   d 9.02   **e** 7.98

2 Give the following numbers correct to 1 s.f.
   a 1621   **b** 349   **c** 5189

3 Give the numbers in question 1 correct to 1 s.f.

Tactics

A zero at the start or end of a number is very important, but not significant. It shows the place value of the other digits. The numbers 2, 20 and 200 are all given to 1 s.f. but, if you are planning a party, you need to know whether to expect 2, 20 or 200 guests, so ignore the zeros at your peril!

Largest and smallest values

If a number has been rounded to 9 to 1 s.f. the largest possible value for that number is 9.5 and the smallest possible value is 8.5.

Normally a number given as 9.5 is rounded up, but to find the largest value, there must be a cut-off point. Should it be 9.4, 9.49, 9.499, 9.4999...? The rule is that the cut-off point is halfway to the next unit.

Example

An answer is given as 12 to the nearest whole number. Give its largest and smallest values.

Draw a number line, with the required number and the integers immediately each side of it, in this case 11 and 13. Draw lines halfway to the numbers on either side of 12 and read off the values as shown.

The smallest value is 11.5 and the largest is 12.5.

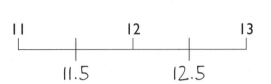

Example

An answer is given as 7.6 to the nearest 0.1. Give its smallest and largest values.

The smallest value is 7.55 and the largest is 7.65.

Example

A crowd at a concert was recorded as 800 to the nearest 100. Give the smallest and largest numbers that could have attended.

The smallest number is 750 and the greatest is 850.

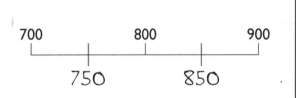

Exercise 2

1 A plank of wood is 4 m long, measured to the nearest metre. What are the shortest and longest lengths that it could be? Give your answers in cm.

2 A toddler's height was measured as 70 cm to the nearest cm. What is the shortest and greatest height that the child could be?

3 A population in a town was estimated at 60 000 to the nearest thousand. What is the smallest and greatest number of people that there could be in the population of that town?

Problems

Understanding the jargon

Estimate   an approximate or rough answer
Draw, construct, measure   follow the appropriate instruction to draw, construct or measure
Calculate, give an exact value for   work out the exact answer from information given, without attempting to draw or measure (Round the answer at the end if necessary.)

Example

$$\frac{3.91 \times 19.7}{10.1 \times 2.3}$$

a   Without using a calculator, give an estimated answer.
b   Use a calculator to work out an exact answer, writing down all the digits on your calculator display.
c   Give your answer correct to 2 s.f.

a $\dfrac{3.91 \times 19.7}{10.1 \times 2.3} \approx \dfrac{4 \times 20}{10 \times 2}$

$\qquad\qquad\quad = \dfrac{80}{20}$

$\qquad\qquad\quad = 4$

b   Use brackets or the memory on your calculator.
$(3.91 \times 19.7) \div (10.1 \times 2.3) = 3.315\,841\,584$

c $3.315\,841\,584 = 3.3$ to 2 s.f.

Remember, scientific calculators always carry out instructions in the following order:

Brackets powers Divide Multiply Add Subtract

Exercise 1

$$\frac{29.8 \times 5.1}{35.2 + 15.4} =$$

1   Look at the question above, and give an approximate answer.
2   Use your calculator to work out the answer, correct to 1 s.f.

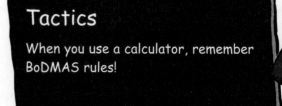

Tactics

When you use a calculator, remember BoDMAS rules!

Understanding the jargon

Show your working   means what it says, you may lose marks if you don't!
Give a reason, explain your answer   in words or symbols, but your reason must be based either on information from the question or previous mathematical knowledge, not a wild guess.

Show your working

Example
Mrs Brown booked four tickets for the theatre, two at £6.50 each and two at £5.25. How much money did she have left over from £50.00? Show your working.

Cost of tickets $= (2 \times £6.50) + (2 \times £5.25)$
$= £13.00 + £10.50$
$= 23.50$
Money left over $= £50.00 - £23.50$
$= £26.50$

You can work out the calculation in different ways, but it is always important to:
*   show the actual calculations
    (e.g. £50.00 − £23.50 = £26.50)
*   explain what the calculations represent in words or symbols
    (e.g. Money left over =).

Give a reason/explain your answer

Example
Three angles of a quadrilateral are 140°, 78° and 37°. What is the fourth angle? Give a reason for your answer.

$140° + 78° + 37° = 255°$
The fourth angle $= 360° - 255°$
$= 105°$ (The angles of a quadrilateral add up to 360°.)

Exercise 2

1   Natalie bought a chocolate bar which had 40 square pieces. She kept $\frac{1}{4}$ of them herself and gave Colin the remaining pieces. Colin ate $\frac{2}{5}$ of his share himself and gave the remaining pieces to Anna. She ate $\frac{1}{2}$ of her share and gave Tim the remainder. Tim kept five pieces and gave the remainder back to Natalie. How many pieces of chocolate did Natalie have at the end?

2   In a class survey, 15% of pupils asked said that they had walked to school that day, 45% came by bus and the rest came by car. What percentage came by car?

Multiplying and dividing fractions and decimals

Understanding the jargon

Integer   whole number
Mixed number   whole number and fraction
Numerator   top number of a fraction
Denominator   bottom number of a fraction
Improper fraction   fraction with the numerator bigger than the denominator (also called a top-heavy fraction)
Cancel/reduce to lowest terms   divide top and bottom by common factors

How to multiply fractions

- Turn mixed numbers into improper fractions, then cancel if possible – one factor from the numerator and one from the denominator each time.
- Multiply along the numerators and multiply along the denominators.
- Change to a mixed number and cancel if necessary.

Examples

- $\frac{3}{10} \times \frac{5}{9} = \frac{1}{2} \times \frac{1}{3} = \frac{1}{6}$
- $2\frac{1}{2} \times 3\frac{1}{4} = \frac{5}{2} \times \frac{13}{4} = \frac{65}{8} = 8\frac{1}{8}$

Example

Find $\frac{1}{4}$ of 100.

$\frac{1}{4}$ of $100 = 100 \times \frac{1}{4} = 25$

How to multiply decimals

- Count the total number of digits after the decimal points.
- There must be the same number of decimal places in the answer as in the question.

Exercise 1

Without working out the answer, choose the correct alternative

1   $12 \times \frac{3}{4}$ is bigger/smaller than 12
    and bigger/smaller than $\frac{3}{4}$.

2   $\frac{3}{5} \times 17$ is bigger/smaller than 17
    and bigger/smaller than $\frac{3}{5}$.

3   $\frac{1}{2} \times \frac{3}{4}$ is bigger/smaller than 1.

Tactics

When you multiply by a number that is greater than 1 your answer is larger than the original amount, but when you multiply by a number that is less than 1 your answer is smaller than your original amount.

Examples

- $0.3 \times 0.2 = 0.06$ 0.3 and 0.2 each have one digit after the point, so there must be two digits after the point in the answer. (i.e. tenths × tenths = hundredths)
- $7 \times 0.2 = 1.4$

How to divide fractions

- Turn mixed numbers into improper fractions.
- Turn the second fraction upside down, and change the sign to a multiplication.
- Proceed as for multiplication.

Example

$$10\tfrac{1}{2} \div 3\tfrac{3}{4} = \tfrac{21}{2} \div \tfrac{15}{4} = \tfrac{21}{2} \times \tfrac{4}{15} = \tfrac{7}{1} \times \tfrac{2}{5} = \tfrac{14}{5}$$
$$= 2\tfrac{4}{5}$$

Example

How many halves make 6?
$$6 \div \tfrac{1}{2} = 6 \times 2$$
$$= 12$$

How to divide decimals

Understanding the jargon

Divisor   number by which you are dividing (In $8 \div 2$ the divisor is 2.)

Example

$$4.08 \div 1.2 = 40.8 \div 12$$
$$= 3.4$$

Example

How many 0.01s in 5?
$$5 \div 0.01 = 500 \div 1$$
$$= 500$$

Exercise 2

Without working out the answers, choose the correct alternative.

1   $4 \div 0.5$ is bigger/smaller than 4.
2   1.2 divided by 3 is bigger/smaller than 3.
3   $0.8 \div 0.2$ is bigger/smaller than 0.8.

Tactics

When you divide by a number that is greater than 1 your answer is smaller than the original amount, but when you divide by a number that is smaller than 1 your answer is greater than your original amount.

13

Proportion and ratio

Proportion

Finding the cost of one

> **Example**
> Eight copies of a book cost £45.60.
> *a* What does one book cost?   *b* What do nine copies cost?
>
> *a* 1 book costs £45.60 ÷ 8 = £5.70   *b* 9 books cost £5.70 × 9 = £51.30

Using amounts other than 1

> **Example**
> A recipe uses 250 grams of margarine to make six cakes.
> *a* How many grams of margarine would you need to make 12 cakes?
> *b* How many grams of margarine would you need to make 9 cakes?
>
> *a* To make 12 cakes (twice the recipe), you will need twice as much margarine.
>   6 cakes   250 grams
>   12 cakes   250 grams × 2 = 500 grams
>   You need 500 grams of margarine for 12 cakes.
>   It is easy to spot that 12 is twice 6, so you will need twice as much margarine.
>   2 is the **multiplier** or **scale factor**.
>
> *b* Six cakes use 250 grams.
>   The multiplier for 9 cakes is 9 ÷ 6 = 1.5.
>
> | Cakes | Margarine |
> |-------|-----------|
> | 6 | 250 grams |
> | × | × |
> | 1.5 | 1.5 |
> | 9 | 375 grams |
>
>   To make nine cakes, use 375 grams of margarine.

Exercise 1

1 12 fruit trees cost £171.00.
   a What would one tree cost?
   b What would ten trees cost?
   c How many trees could you buy
      for £256.50?

2 A recipe uses four eggs to make 24 cakes.
   Work out how many eggs you would need
   to make:
   a 12 cakes   b 8 cakes   c 6 cakes
   d 16 cakes.

Tactics

To find a multiplier or scale
factor, divide the new amount
(what you need to know) by the
old (what you know already).

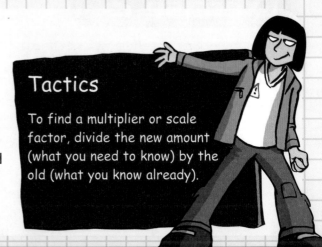

Ratio

Exercise 2

Mr Grant is planning to grow vegetables in his garden. He thinks that he will use twice as much of his garden for vegetables as he will for flowers.

1 What is the ratio of vegetable garden to flower garden?
2 If he uses 60 m^2 of his garden for vegetables, how many square metres will he use for flowers?
3 How big are the flower and vegetable gardens altogether?
4 If he decides instead to divide his garden in the ratio of 3 : 2, vegetable garden to flower garden, how many square metres will he have for each part?

Tactics

Scale factors are novel!
They are New OVEr oLd .

15

How to tackle coursework

By now you may well have had your first taste of coursework, either in maths or in other subjects. Certainly, in year 10, coursework starts to kick in, as a good coursework grade can give you a flying start in your GCSE.

- As soon as a piece of coursework is set, write down the date that it is due in. It's also a good idea to make a reminder for yourself for about a week before the deadline so that you aren't frantically trying to cram a month's work into a few hectic hours the night before. It's useful if you can space it out, especially if you are juggling several pieces, but that depends very much on how it's set and it may be beyond your control. If you do get bogged down, remember, the most important piece of coursework is the one that's due in next. Teachers will sometimes give you an extension on the time, but you need to have a good reason for asking, and they won't be sympathetic if you make a habit of missing deadlines. If you're usually reliable, though, they may take pity on you in an emergency.

- For many subjects, you need to do some research. You may have suitable books at home but, if not, you can use the school or public library or – if you have access to it – the Internet. Many schools will let you go on-line during the lunch break or after school, so you should be able to manage if you need to.

- Whatever you do, don't just copy out chunks from books, or download pages from the Web and try to pass them off as your own. Teachers aren't fools, despite what you might think, and they have an uncanny ability to spot this sort of thing. You can quote directly if it seems appropriate, provided that you make clear that you are doing so and state the source of your information. Otherwise, you must write everything in your own words.

- You don't normally have to do much external research for maths coursework. Usually you are set either a practical task or an investigation. For a practical task you might be asked to redesign your bedroom or plan a holiday. An investigation may involve working out the number of painted faces on a cube, or the number of rhombuses you can draw in a given shape. It's likely that you will have to do at least four pieces of coursework, two of each type, before the end of year 11.

- Whatever the coursework topic, it's important that you set it out well. Even if handwriting isn't your strong point, try at least to be legible. Rulers are cheap enough so you have no excuse for not using one to underline or draw columns. Computer-produced spreadsheets, graphs and tables can look very professional but find out the rules and regulations about using computers beforehand, as they change from year to year.

- Whatever the coursework, it's how you use the maths that is important. If you have to design a kitchen then think how you can introduce:
  - number: costing, percentage of budget for various items, ratio and proportion in allocating space for different uses
  - space: area and perimeter, circles if you investigate whether a circular kitchen table would fit in the space, possibly angles when you work out the height and accessibility of appliances
  - data: recording the opinions and preferences of the people who are going to use the kitchen.

  These are just a few ideas to get you started. The important thing is, though, that they all involve maths. Making a scrapbook of pictures cut from DIY catalogues doesn't!

- Investigations are usually more algebra-based. You will probably be given an example to test – such as the number of matchsticks used in making a shape – and asked to investigate. Start by answering any questions that you are given.

- You often have first to test the information and show that it's correct, then 'investigate'. When you get to this part, it's usually a good idea to start with the simplest possible number: 'How many matchsticks do I need for pattern 1?', for instance. Then see what happens for pattern 2 and so on, making one change at a time.

- Set out the results in tables and you should see a pattern emerging. Try to work out rules for any patterns that you find. Write them in symbols if you can, but if you're not sure how to do this, ask your teacher for help, or write the formula in words.

- To get even more marks, try to figure out why the rule works, then extend the investigation. If your rule works for squares, for example, see if it holds for rectangles, and if not, what modifications you need and why. Start with the simplest example and make changes, one at a time.

Simplifying algebra

Multiplying and dividing – getting the right sign

Remember! $+ \times + = +$ $+ \times - = -$
            $- \times - = +$ $- \times + = -$

Same plus

Examples

- $2d + 5d = 7d$
- $3t - 8t = -5t$
- $3y \times 2y = 6y^2$ (Remember to multiply both parts.)
- $3c + 3c^2 = 3c + 3c^2$ (You can't mix c and c^2.)
- $8w \div 2w = 4$

Example

Simplify the expression $3x + 6y - 5x + 2xy + 2y$.
It's often easier to rearrange the expression, putting like with like.
Tick the terms as you write them so that you don't leave any out.
$3x - 5x + 6y + 2y + 2xy$
  $- 2x$ $+ 8y$ $+ 2xy$ $3x + 6y - 5x + 2xy + 2y = -2x + 8y + 2xy$

Simplifying single brackets

Examples

Simplify these.

a $2(z + 4) \rightarrow 2 (z + 4) \rightarrow 2 \times z + 2 \times 4 = 2z + 8$

b $-2(z - 4) \rightarrow -2 (z - 4) \rightarrow -2 \times z + -2 \times -4 = -2z + 8$

(Remember, a minus times a minus is a plus.)

c $2(z - 4) \rightarrow 2 (z - 4) \rightarrow 2 \times z + 2 \times -4 = 2z - 8$

d $-2(z + 4) \rightarrow -2 (z + 4) \rightarrow -2 \times z + -2 \times 4 = -2z - 8$

If you find this hard, split the problem up. Work out the result of multiplying the numbers or letters, and then work out which sign to put.

Example

$2r + 5(3r - 6) - 4(r - 3)$
$= 2r + 15r - 30 - 4r + 12$
$= 2r + 15r - 4r - 30 + 12$
$= 2r + 15r - 4r - 18$

Exercise 1

Simplify these expressions.
1 $6a + 2b - 3a + 5b$
2 $3f + 5g + 6f - 8g$
3 $3m + 2m^2 - 6m^2 + m$ (Remember: $m = 1m$)

Exercise 2

Simplify these expressions.
1 **a** $14x - 2g - 3x + 7g$ **b** $5y^2 + 2y^2 + 3y - 2xy$
2 **a** $3(5h + 2j - 4c^2)$ **b** $5(d - 2) - 3(d + 2)$

Tactics

If the signs are the same, you end up with a plus, but if they're different, you don't.

You can write the terms in any order as long as the signs are right.

RED ALERT!   You can only add or subtract like with like.   RED

How to multiply out and simplify double brackets . . .

. . . using FOIL

FOIL stands for First Outside Inside Last.
It gives you an easy way of multiplying every
pair without leaving any out or multiplying
any pair twice.

Example

Simplify $(y + 3)(y + 2)$ $(y + 3)(y + 2)$

First	Outside	Inside	Last
$y \times y$	$y \times 2$	$3 \times y$	3×2
y^2	$+ 2y$	$+ 3y$	$+ 6$

$(y + 3)(y + 2) = y^2 + 2y + 3y + 6 = y^2 + 5y + 6$

Example

Simplify $(w + 2)(w - 5)$

First	Outside	Inside	Last
$w \times w$	$w \times -5$	$2 \times w$	2×-5
w^2	$-5w$	$+ 2w$	-10

$(w + 2)(w - 5) = w^2 - 5w + 2w - 10$
$\qquad\qquad\quad = w^2 - 3w - 10$

Example

Simplify $(t - 6)(t - 2)$
$(t - 6)(t - 2) = t^2 - 2t - 6t + 12$
$(-6 \times -2 = +12)$
$t^2 - 2t - 6t + 12 = t^2 - 8t + 12$

. . . using a grid

Example

Simplify $(y + 3)(y + 2)$

$\times$	y	$+ 3$
y	y^2	$+ 3y$
$+ 2$	$+ 2y$	$+ 6$

$(y + 3)(y + 2) = y^2 + 2y + 3y + 6$
$\qquad\qquad\quad = y^2 + 5y + 6$

Example

Simplify $(w + 2)(w - 5)$

$\times$	w	$+ 2$
w	w^2	$+ 2w$
-5	$- 5w$	$- 10$

$(w + 2)(w - 5) = w^2 - 5w + 2w - 10$
$\qquad\qquad\quad = w^2 - 3w - 10$

Example

Simplify $(t - 6)(t - 2)$

$\times$	t	$- 6$
t	t^2	$- 6t$
-2	$- 2t$	$+ 12$

$(t - 6)(t - 2) = t^2 - 2t - 6t + 12$
$\qquad\qquad\quad = t^2 - 8t + 12$

Exercise 3

Simplify these expressions.

1 $(x + 6)(x + 3)$ 2 $(b + 2)(b - 4)$
3 $(p - 3)(p + 2)$ 4 $(d - 4)(d - 1)$

Exercise 4

Simplify these expressions, using whichever
method you prefer.

1 $(x - 3)(x - 8)$ 2 $(e + 2)(e - 7)$
3 $(a - 4)(a + 5)$ 4 $(y + 10)(y + 3)$

Tactics

Be very careful with signs.
Remember a sign sticks to the
number or letter which comes
immediately after it. If there is no
sign written in front of the number
or letter it is treated as positive.

19

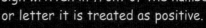

Most teachers use either the **FOIL** or the grid method.
Choose whichever applies to you.

RED ALERT

Simultaneous equations

Understanding the jargon

Variable   a letter which changes in value: in $6x$, the variable is x

Simultaneous equations   two or more equations that are true for all variables but have one pair of solutions that works for both equations

Checking up on equations

$x + 4 = 7$	$\rightarrow \quad x = 7 - 4$	$\rightarrow \; x = 3$
$y - 2 = 10$	$\rightarrow \quad y = 10 + 2$	$\rightarrow \; y = 12$
$2w + 3 = 17$	$\rightarrow \; 2w = 17 - 3 = 14$	$\rightarrow \; w = 14 \div 2 = 7$
$3r - 4 = 11$	$\rightarrow \quad 3r = 11 + 4 = 15$	$\rightarrow \; r = 15 \div 3 = 5$

Solving simultaneous equations by elimination

This is the most common algebraic method, and is the only one covered in this book. Each variable must be worth the same amount whenever it appears in each equation. The aim is to eliminate, or 'get rid of' one variable at a time.

Example

$5x + 6y = 45$ (1) ⎫ The only difference
$5x + 2y = 25$ (2) ⎬ between these is an
$\qquad\qquad\qquad$ ⎭ extra $4y$ in (1).
$\qquad 4y = 20$ Subtract the equations.
$\qquad\; y = 5$ $(1) - (2)$
$5x + 30 = 45$ ⎫ Substitute $y = 5$ in one of
$\quad 5x = 15$ ⎬ the original equations.
$\qquad x = 3$ ⎭ $5x + 6 \times 5 = 5x + 30$
Check your answer by substituting $x = 3$, $y = 5$ into equation (2).
$5 \times 3 + 2 \times 5 = 25$

Example

$7x + 3y = 38$ (1) ⎫ You have $3y$ in each
$\qquad\qquad\qquad\qquad$ ⎬ equation.
$2x + 3y = 13$ (2) ⎭ $(1) - (2)$
$\qquad 5x = 25$
$\qquad\; x = 5$
Substitute $x = 5$ into equation (1).
$35 + 3y = 38 \rightarrow 3y = 3 \rightarrow y = 1$
Check by substituting in (2).
$2 \times 5 + 3 \times 1 = 13$

Exercise 1

Solve these simultaneous equations.

1 $3x + 2y = 22$
$\quad$ $3x + y = 14$

2 $5x + 4y = 62$
$\quad$ $2x + 4y = 32$

3 $4x + 3y = 63$
$\quad$ $2x + 3y = 39$

Tactics

You can multiply all the way across an equation and still have a correct answer.

For example, if $x = 3$ and $y = 5$ then
$3x + 2y = 19$ $\quad$ and $\quad$ $6x + 4y = 38$
$\quad 9 + 10 = 19$ $\qquad\qquad$ $18 + 20 = 38$

You may have to multiply to make the number multiplying the variables the same in both equations.

Example

$2x + 5y = 23$ (1) $\times 2$ to give $10y$ in each equation.
$3x + 10y = 42$ (2)
$4x + 10y = 46$ (3)   (You must multiply every term in the equation to keep it right.)
      $x = 4$ (3) − (2)
Substitute $x = 4$ in (1). (It doesn't matter which equation you use.)
   $8 + 5y = 23$
      $5y = 15$
        $y = 3$
Check in (2):
$3 \times 4 + 10 \times 3 = 42$

Sometimes you have to multiply both equations.

Example

Solve these simultaneous equations.
   $3x + 4y = 40$
   $2x + 5y = 43$

Either: *Or:*

Either			Or		
$3x + 4y = 40$	(1)	$\times 2$ } to give $6x$ in	$3x + 4y = 40$	(1)	$\times 5$ } to give $20y$ in
$2x + 5y = 43$	(2)	$\times 3$ } both equations.	$2x + 5y = 43$	(2)	$\times 4$ } both equations.
$6x + 8y = 80$	(3)		$15x + 20y = 200$	(3)	
$6x + 15y = 129$	(4)		$8x + 20y = 172$	(4)	
$7y = 49$	(4) − (3)		$7x = 28$	(3) − (4)	
$y = 7$			$x = 4$		

Substitute $y = 7$ in (1).   Substitute $x = 4$ in (2).
   $3x + 28 = 40$ $8 + 5y = 43$
      $3x = 12$ $5y = 35$
        $x = 4$ $y = 7$
Check in (2): $2 \times 4 + 5 \times 7 = 43$

Exercise 2

Solve these simultaneous equations.

1 $10x + 3y = 60$
     $5x + 7y = 85$

2 $2x + 3y = 17$
     $7x + 5y = 32$

Tactics

You can add or subtract equations as long as you keep the equals sign in the right place. You are adding the same amount to both sides of the equation.

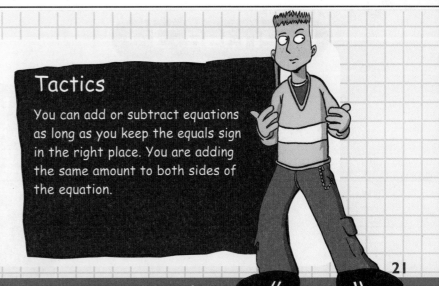

ERT RED ALERT RED ALERT! RED ALERT RED ALERT

So far, all the solutions have involved subtracting one equation from another. Sometimes, however, you have to add the equations.

Example

$3x + 5y = 20$ (1)
$2x - 5y = 5$ (2)

Subtracting these equations gives:

$3x - 2x = x$
and $5y - -5y = 5y + 5y = 10y$.
The new equation is $x + 10y = 15$.

Although this is still correct, it isn't very helpful.
You still have an x-term and a y-term.

When the signs of the variable you want to cancel out are different, add the equations.
Remember that $+5y + -5y = 0$

$3x + 5y = 20$ (1)
$2x - 5y = 5$ (2)
    $5x = 25$ (1) + (2)
      $x = 5$

Substitute $x = 5$ in (1).
  $15 + 5y = 20$
      $5y = 5$
       $y = 1$

Check in (2):
$2 \times 5 - 5 \times 1 = 5$

If you have a choice of eliminating a positive or a negative term, try to eliminate the negative.

Exercise 3

Solve these simultaneous equations.

1 $3x + 2y = 28$
    $7x - 2y = 32$
2 $8x - 3y = 68$
    $3x + 3y = 42$

Tactics

When the signs of the variable you want to eliminate are the same, subtract. When they are different, add.

You can still subtract your equations, even if you have negative signs in front of the variables that you are going to eliminate.

Example

$7x - 2y = 40$ (1)
$3x - 2y = 16$ (2)
You can subtract these equations, because $-2y - -2y = -2y + 2y = 0$.
$7x - 2y = 40$ (1)
$3x - 2y = 16$ (2)
$\qquad 4x = 24$ (1) − (2)
$\qquad\ x = 6$
Substitute $x = 6$ in (1).
$42 - 2y = 40$
$\quad -2y = 40 - 42 = -2$
$\quad\ -y = -1$
$\qquad y = 1$
Check in (2):
$3 \times 6 - 2 \times 1 = 16$

Simultaneous equations in a nutshell

- Decide which variable to eliminate and make sure that the numbers multiplying them are the same in each line, regardless of sign. Multiply one or both if necessary.
- If the signs are the same, subtract the equations, if one is positive and one negative, add the equations.
- Substitute the value you have found into one of the original equations to find the value of the other variable.
- Check that both values work in the remaining equation.

Exercise 4

Solve these simultaneous equations.

1 $6x - 2y = 6$
   $10x - 2y = 14$
2 $4x + 3y = 19$
   $15x - 3y = 0$
3 $5x - 4y = 27$
   $2x - 4y = 6$

Tactics

STOP! Do you add or subtract the equations?
Same Take: if the signs of the variables to be eliminated are the same (both positive or both negative) subtract.
Opposite Plus: if the signs of the variables to be eliminated are opposite (one positive and one negative) add.
Same Take Opposite Plus

ERT   **Solutions to equations may be negative, fractional or both.**   RED ALERT

Solving simultaneous equations with graphs

Sometimes it is easier to use a graph to solve simultaneous equations.

Example

The graph shows the equations $y = 2x + 4$ and $y = x + 6$.
From the graph solve the simultaneous equations:
$y = 2x + 4$
$y = x + 6$
Both these equations are equal to y, so
$2x + 4 = x + 6$.
The answer is at the point where the graphs cross.
$x = 2, y = 8$

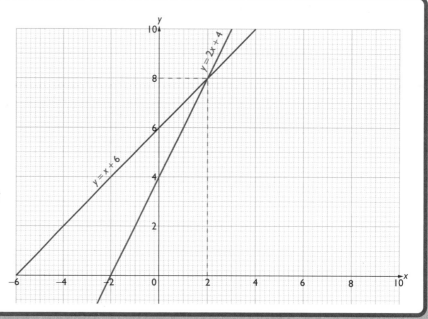

Sometimes the equations may be arranged slightly differently, but the answer is always at the point of intersection, i.e. where the lines cross.

Exercise 5

Use the graph to solve these simultaneous equations.
Hint: Find the intersection of each pair of lines.

1 $y = 2x$
    $y = 6 - x$

2 $y = x + 4$
    $y = 2x$

3 $y = 6 - x$
    $y = x + 4$

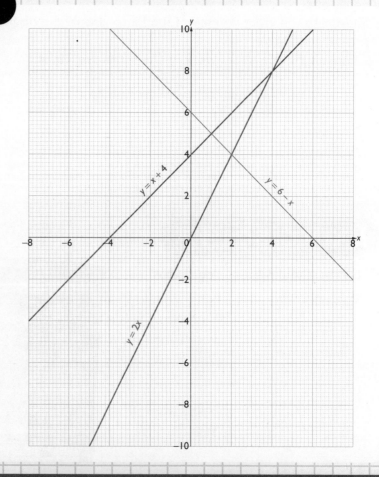

24

Sometimes you are given the simultaneous equations and have to draw the graph.

Example

By drawing a suitable graph, solve the following simultaneous equations.

$y = 2x + 1$
$y = 4 - x$

Start by making tables of values.

$y = 2x + 1$					
x	−2	−1	0	1	2
$2x$	−4	−2	0	2	4
$+1$	$+1$	$+1$	$+1$	$+1$	$+1$
y	−3	−1	1	3	5

$y = 4 - x$					
x	−2	−1	0	1	2
y	6	5	4	3	2

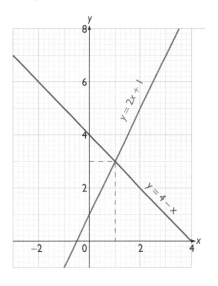

Then draw the graphs as shown.
Always extend the lines to the edge of your graph.

You should see that the lines cross at (1, 3).
$x = 1, y = 3$

Exercise 6

Complete these tables of values.

$y = x + 3$					
x	−2	−1	0	1	2
y	1		3		

$y = 2x + 4$					
x	−2	−1	0	1	2
y	0	2		6	

Draw an x-axis with values from −2 to 2.
Draw a y-axis with values from −6 to 10.
Plot the points of the equations and hence solve the simultaneous equations:
$y = x + 3$
$y = 2x + 4$

Tactics

Always use a ruler and a really sharp pencil when you are drawing straight-line graphs.

25

Graphs, lines,equations

The line $x = 4$ is a vertical line passing through $(4, 0)$.
For every point on the line, the y-value changes but $x = 4$.
The line $y = -2$ is a horizontal line passing through $(0, -2)$. For every point on the line, the x-value changes, but $y = -2$.
The line $y = x$ is a line passing through $(0, 0)$ at $45°$ to the x-axis.
The line $y = x - 4$ is parallel to $y = x$ and passes through the y-axis at $(0, -4)$.
The line $y = x + 4$ is parallel to $y = x$ and passes through the y-axis at $(0, 4)$.
A line $y = \frac{1}{2}x + 3$ would cut the y-axis at $(0, 3)$.
A line $y = 100x - 2$ would cut the y-axis at $(0, -2)$.
If $x = 0$, then $\frac{1}{2}x$, $100x$ or any multiple of x is 0.

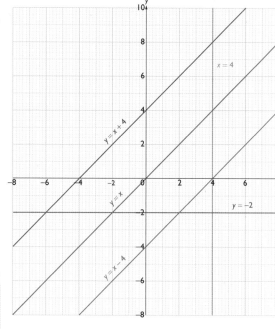

Example
At which point do the following lines cut the y-axis?
a $y = 2x - 1$ $(0, -1)$ b $y = 3.6x + 0.5$ $(0, 0.5)$

Exercise 1

Fill in the gaps to show which line has which equation.

1   Line _____ has equation $y = x$.
2   Line _____ has equation $x = 3$.
3   Line _____ has equation $y = \frac{1}{2}x + 4$.
4   Line _____ has equation $y = -4$.
5   Line _____ has equation $y = \frac{1}{2}x - 4$.

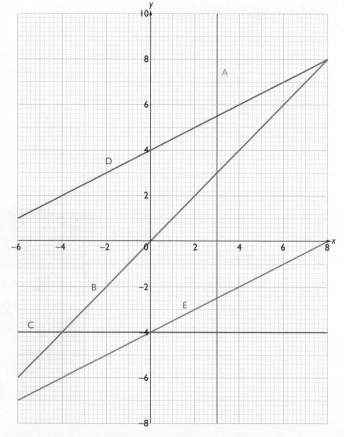

How to work out if a point is on a given line

Example
Is the point (2, 6) on the line
$y = x + 4$?
Substitute the values $x = 2$ and $y = 6$ into the equation.
$6 = 2 + 4$
This is correct, so (2, 6) is on the line.

Example
Is the point (3, 10) on the line $y = 2x + 5$?
Substitute the values $x = 3$ and $y = 10$ into the equation.
$10 = 2 \times 3 + 5 = 11$
This is wrong as 10 cannot equal 11, so the point is not on the line.

Example
A line with the equation $y = ax + 6$ passes through the point (3, 12).
What is the value of a and what is the complete equation?
Substitute $x = 3$ and $y = 12$.
$12 = 3a + 6$
$3a = 12 - 6$
$3a = 6$
$a = 2$
The equation is $y = 2x + 6$.

Exercise 2

1 a   Is the point (5, 17) on the line $y = 3x + 1$?
   b   Is the point (2, 13) on the line $y = 2x + 9$?
2 A line with the equation $y = bx - 5$ passes through the point (8, 11).
   What is the value of b and what is the complete equation?

Tactics

You can draw dotted lines on your graph, to show your working, as on page 25. Then even if your answer is wrong, you may get some marks for your method.

Inequalities

To solve inequalities, you need to understand the following signs.

< is less than   > is greater than

≤ is less than or equal to   ≥ is greater than or equal to

$w < 6$ means w can take any value up to 5.999 99… but not exactly 6.

$w ≤ 6$ means that w can take any value up to and including 6.

$w > 6$ means that w can be 6.0… but cannot be exactly 6.

$w ≥ 6$ means that x can be exactly 6, or take any value above 6.

Be careful when using negative numbers. remember $4 < 6$,

but $-4 > -6$.

How to solve questions using inequalities

Examples

- x is an integer (whole number) such that $x < 5$.
  What is the largest possible value of x?
  Since x must be a whole number less than 5, the greatest possible value is 4.
- y is an integer such that $y < 5$ and $y ≥ 1$.
  What values could y take?
  Since y must be a whole number, at least 1 and less than 5, it can only be 1, 2, 3 or 4.

Usually inequalities behave just like equations, but there are two exceptions.

The inequality swaps round when:

- all the terms on one side of the inequality swap sides with all terms on the other side

- both sides of an inequality are multiplied by a negative number.

Example

$7 > x$ so $x < 7$

This is sometimes easier to understand using a real-life example.

A giraffe > a flea and a flea < a giraffe.

Examples

- $-z > -3$ so $z < 3$
Try this with other numbers to see if it always works.
- $-5 > -9$ $-5 × -1 = 5$ $-9 × -1 = 9$
  $5 < 9$
- $-4 < 2$ Multiply both sides of the inequality by -1 and the result is $4 > -2$.

Exercise 1

Put in < or > to make the inequality correct.

1   5 ____ 6   2   -2 ____ -3

3   8 ____ 2   4   -10 ____ -4

Tactics

Inequalities behave very much like equations.

Exercise 2

1   Solve these inequalities.

    a $3s < 12$ b $5s - 1 ≥ 9$ c $2d > 16$

2   In each of the following questions, x is an integer.

    a   Give the largest value for x when $x < 5$.   b $x > 3$ and $x < 6$. What values could x take?

Sequences

Example

5, 9, 13, 17, …
a   Find the next two numbers in the sequence.
b   How do you find the next term in this sequence?
c   The formula for the nth term of this sequence is $t = 4n + 1$. Find the 30th term.
d   Is the number 241 part of this sequence?
a   21, 25
b   Add 4 to the previous number in the sequence.
c $4 \times 30 + 1 = 121$
d $4n + 1 = 241 \rightarrow 4n = 240 \rightarrow n = 60$
    Yes, the number 241 is the 60th term.

Not all sequences are formed by adding or subtracting the same amount each time.

Example

Find the next two terms of the following sequence.

Number, n	1		2		3		4	5	6
Term, t	1		4		9		16	…	…
Differences		3		5		7			

The differences between the terms are 3, 5, 7, …
The differences are increasing by 2 each time. The next two numbers will be 25 and 36.

If you recognise that the first term is 1^2, the second is 2^2, the third is 3^2 and so on, you can work out the fifth as being 5^2 and the 6th as 6^2. The formula is $t = n^2$.

Example

Number, n	1	2	3	4	5	
Term, t	2	5	10	17	…	The nth term is $n^2 + 1$.
Term, t	6	9	14	21	…	The nth term is $n^2 + 5$.

Exercise 1

The formula for a sequence is $t = 2n - 3$.

1   Find the first three terms.
2   Is the number 502 part of this sequence?
3   The formula for the nth term of a sequence is $t = n^2 + 10$.
    Which of the following numbers are in the sequence?
    16, 35, 59, 71, 100
4   The formula for a sequence is $t = 2n^2$.
    a   Work out the first four numbers of the sequence.
    b   What do you notice about the differences between the numbers?

3

Getting ready for year 10

You are now well on in your secondary school career, and next year you will start preparing for GCSE. Over the next few weeks and months you will have to do some hard thinking about the subjects that you are going to keep and those that you are going to drop. Some subjects are compulsory, and the others are usually arranged in 'pools' so that you choose one from each pool. This lets you keep your options open as far as possible. Most people don't know at this stage what they want to do once they have left school or college, and, also, you need to be able to change your mind if circumstances change or you go off your earlier idea. However, you will have some choices open, so here are a few ideas for you to think about.

• Choose subjects you enjoy and at which you can succeed, and not because you want to be with your best friend, or you do or don't like the teacher. Best friends and teachers move, so don't rely on the situation at the start of year 10 being the same right through to the end of year 11.

• If you do have any ideas about a career, find out if there are any subjects that you absolutely must have. Unless you are going to be a professional musician or athlete, you can probably safely drop almost anything at this stage and take it up again later if you need it. If you are interested in doing something artistic, you'll probably choose art anyway, and you won't be allowed to drop English, maths or science, so you won't miss out on the basics.

- Find out what the syllabus involves. Your school will probably have special sessions for your age group. Talk to other people in years 10 and 11 about what the subject involves, but don't be totally persuaded by them one way or the other. It's your life, remember!

Here are a few more ideas worth bearing in mind.

- If you hate reading, or writing essays, think twice about a subject like history.
- If you love PE, remember that there is a great deal of theory, and sporting skill alone won't get you a good mark.
- Do you get in a state over exams and feel less pressured when you can take your time? If so, a subject that is coursework-orientated will suit you better.
- Do you hate having coursework deadlines hanging over you? You'd rather get it over with in one go? It's probably an exam-based option for you.

Pythagoras' theorem

Understanding the jargon

Hypotenuse   the longest side of a right-angled triangle, always opposite the right angle

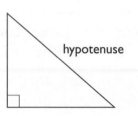
hypotenuse

Sometimes the triangle is turned round, so it is not so easy to spot it.

Pythagoras' theorem (or rule) states that the square on the hypotenuse equals the sum of the squares on the two remaining sides. This means that you could fit squares drawn on the two shorter sides into the area of a square drawn on the longest side. However, we don't usually need to draw squares to use the theorem.

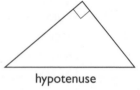
hypotenuse

You will probably see the theorem written in a form like this:
$a^2 + b^2 = c^2$

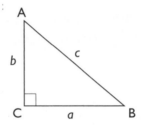

Example

Triangle DEF, which is not drawn accurately, is right-angled at E. DE = 4.2 cm and EF = 6.8 cm.
Find the length of DF.
Using Pythagoras' theorem:
$DF^2 = DE^2 + EF^2 = 4.2^2 + 6.8^2 = 63.88$
$DF = \sqrt{63.88} = 7.99 = 8.0$ cm to 1 d.p.

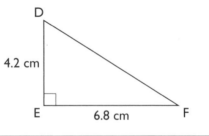

Exercise 1

Triangle PQR is right-angled at Q.
Find the length of PR if:

1   PQ = 7.8 cm and RQ = 2.6 cm.
2   PQ = 9.1 cm and RQ = 3.9 cm.

You may find it helpful to sketch the triangle and mark the right angle and the measurements.

Tactics

The hypotenuse is the longest side in any right-angled triangle.

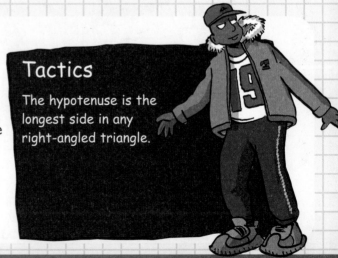

Pythagorean triples

When the lengths of all three sides of a right-angled triangle are integers (whole numbers), they are sometimes called Pythagorean triples. You don't have to learn them, but they can be useful to spot.

> ### Example
> ### *The 3, 4, 5 triangle*
> In triangle ABC, work out the length of the hypotenuse AB when AC = 3 units and BC = 4 units.
> $$c^2 = a^2 + b^2$$
> $$AB^2 = 4^2 + 3^2$$
> $$= 16 + 9$$
> $$= 25$$
> $$AB = \sqrt{25} = 5$$
> AC = 3 units, BC = 4 units, AB = 5 units

This relationship still works when the lengths are multiplied by a scale factor.

> ### Example
> ### *The 6, 8, 10 triangle*
> $$6^2 + 8^2 = 36 + 64$$
> $$= 100$$
> $$\sqrt{100} = 10$$

Often, though, the answers to questions involving Pythagoras' theorem will appear on your calculator as lengthy decimals. When deciding how to round, use the question as a clue and round the answer to the same number.

Exercise 2

1 The lengths of the shorter sides of a right-angled triangle are 5 cm and 12 cm.
   Find the length of the hypotenuse.

2 a How long would the hypotenuse of a right-angled triangle be if the lengths of the other two sides were 12 cm and 16 cm? (Use the information about 3, 4, 5 triangles, above.)
   b What is the scale factor of the enlargement?

Tactics

The right angle is always opposite the hypotenuse.

ERT RED ALERT RED ALERT! RED ALERT RED ALERT

The lengths of the shorter sides

You can use Pythagoras' theorem to find the length of any side of a right-angled triangle, provided that you know the lengths of the other two sides.

$5^2 = 3^2 + 4^2$ To find the hypotenuse, add the squares of the other two sides, and then take the square root.

$25 = 9 + 16$

$9 = 25 - 16$ To find a shorter side, subtract the squares, and then take the square root.

$a^2 + b^2 = c^2$

$\quad b^2 = c^2 - a^2$

$\quad b = \sqrt{c^2 - a^2}$

$\quad a^2 = c^2 - b^2$

$\quad a = \sqrt{c^2 - b^2}$

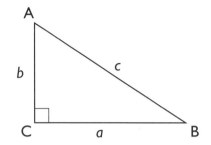

Example

Use Pythagoras' theorem to calculate the length of JK. The diagram is not drawn accurately.

$JK^2 = HK^2 - HJ^2$

$\quad = 11.9^2 - 3.2^2$

$\quad = 131.37$

$\sqrt{131.37} = 11.5$ to 1 d.p.

$JK = 11.5$ cm to 1 d.p.

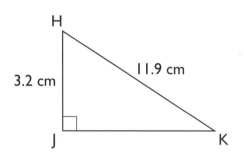

Exercise 3

1   The length of the hypotenuse of a right-angled triangle is 30.5 cm. One of the other sides is 22.3 cm long. Find the length of the third side.

2   The length of the hypotenuse of a right-angled triangle is 20.4 cm. One of the other sides is 7.9 cm long. Peter said that the third side was 21.9 cm. How do you know that this was wrong? What is the right answer?

RED ALERT!   An **E** or **Error** sign on your calculator probably means that you have subtracted the larger square from the smaller square and then tried to find the square root of a negative number.   **RED**

Pythagorean pitfalls

- You **must** have a right-angled triangle before you can use Pythagoras' theorem.
- Add the squares to find the hypotenuse. (ASH)
  Subtract the squares for the other sides. (SOS)
- When subtracting, begin with the bigger number and subtract the smaller.
- Be careful to choose the hypotenuse correctly.

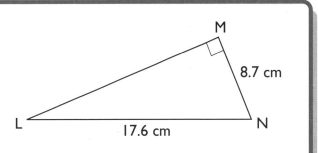

Example
Find the length of LM.
Because LM and LN are almost the same length on the diagram, it would be easy to assume (wrongly) that LM is the hypotenuse.

$$LM^2 = LN^2 - MN^2$$
$$= 17.6^2 - 8.7^2$$
$$= 234.07$$
$$LM = \sqrt{234.07} = 15.3 \text{ cm}$$

Checklist for Pythagoras:

- ☑ Is the triangle right-angled?
- ☑ Do you know the length of the other two sides?
- ☑ Should you add or subtract the squares?

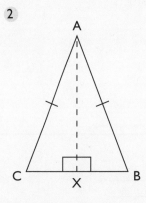

Exercise 4

1 Work out the length of JL. Triangle JKL has not been drawn accurately.

2 Triangle ABC is isosceles. AX bisects (cuts in half) CB and is perpendicular (at right angles) to it.
   The length of AB is 15 cm and the length of AX is 12 cm.
   a Find the length of BX.
   b Find the length of CB.

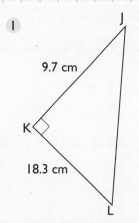

Enlargements

An enlargement is a transformation in which all the lengths of the original shape are multiplied by the same number, called the scale factor, to produce the new shape.

The new shape or point reached after a transformation is often called the image.

You can find the centre of an enlargement by drawing.

Join each point in the original drawing to its image point as shown. Two or more of the lines formed will meet at the centre of the enlargement.

Each line of the image triangle is twice as long as its original.

The scale factor is 2.

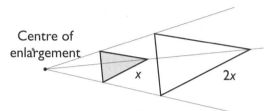

Sometimes an image is smaller than its original. Even so, the transformation is still called an enlargement.

Each length of the original has been halved, or divided by 2, but enlargement scale factors are always found by multiplying, so the scale factor in this case is $\frac{1}{2}$.

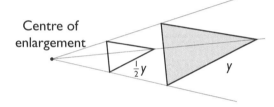

Exercise 1

Triangle ABC has been enlarged to form triangle A'B'C'. Find the centre and the scale factor of the enlargement.

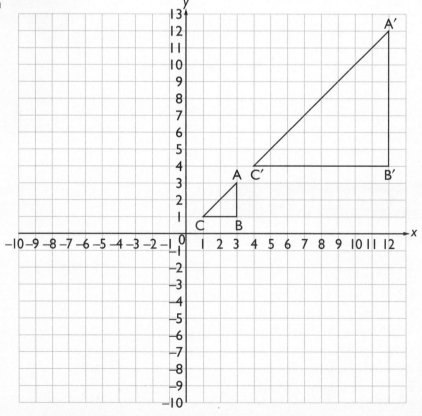

We always read across the graph, the x coordinate, before we read up or down for the y coordinate.

How to find scale factors without measuring

You can find scale factors if you know two lengths, one on the original shape and the corresponding one on its image.

> **Example**
> Triangle DEF has sides of length 3 cm, 4 cm and 5 cm.
> It is enlarged so that the hypotenuse of the image is 17.5 cm. Find the lengths of the other two sides.
> First find the scale factor by dividing the new length by the original length.
> Scale factor = 17.5 ÷ 5 = 3.5
> The lengths of the other two sides are 3 × 3.5 = 10.5 cm and 4 × 3.5 cm = 14 cm.

> **Example**
> The coordinates of point P on a hexagon are (6, 5). It is transformed by an enlargement centred on the origin and the coordinates of its image P′ are (3, 2.5). What is the scale factor of the enlargement?
> Choose either the *x*- or *y*-coordinate.
> Original *x*-coordinate = 6.
> New *x*-coordinate = 3. Scale factor (New OVEr oLd) = 3 ÷ 6 = 0.5
> Scale factor = 0.5. Check the *y*-coordinate: 2.5 ÷ 5 = 0.5

Exercise 2

1 The rectangle RSTU is transformed by an enlargement centred on the origin, scale factor $\frac{1}{2}$. Draw the enlarged shape and label the vertices (corners) R′S′T′U′. What are the coordinates of S′?

2 If the point R moved to (1, 2) under an enlargement centred on the origin, what would be the scale factor of the enlargement?

3 What would be the scale factor of an enlargement centred on the origin to return rectangle R′S′T′U′ to rectangle RSTU?

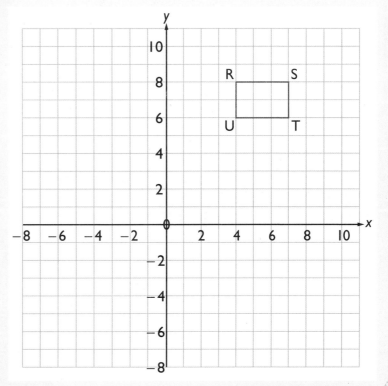

Constructions and loci

Understanding the jargon

Locus of a point   the path that a point follows in response to a rule
Loci   the plural form of locus
Bisect   cut in half
Perpendicular   at right angles

Example
A point P is always 2 m from a fixed point O. What is the locus of point P?
Imagine yourself standing at O, holding a stick 2 m long. Your friend is holding the other end.
What path could your friend travel?
The locus is a circle, centred at O with radius 2 m.

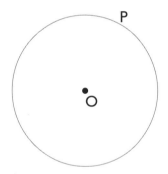

Scale – 1 cm represents 1 m

Example
AB is a line 6 cm long.
What is the locus of a point which is always equidistant (the same distance) from A and B?

Drawn half size

A ——————— B
       6 cm

The locus is the perpendicular bisector of AB.

Example
The lines DE and EF meet at E as shown.
What is the locus of a point which is always equidistant from DE and EF?

D
    E
F

The locus is a line bisecting ∠DEF.

Exercise 1

1   A line RS is 24 cm long. What is the locus of point P, such that PR = PS?

2   What is the locus of a point P which is always 7 cm from a fixed point H?

3   The lines QR and SR meet at angle QRS. Describe the locus of a point which moves so that QR = SR.

Tactics

Always leave construction lines on your diagram, so that your teacher or the examiner can see how you reached your answer.

Loci in practical situations

Example

The diagram shows a field in which a goat is tethered to a post, S, by a rope 2 m long.
Using a scale of 1 cm to represent 2 m, mark the region where the goat may graze.

The locus is a circle of radius 2 m, centred at S.
Shade in the appropriate area as shown, and state the scale used.

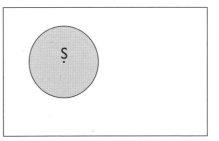

Scale – I cm represents 2 m

Example

A mobile phone mast is to be erected at a point equidistant from farmhouses Q and R. By drawing a suitable line on the diagram, show where the mast could be sited.
The mast could be sited anywhere along the perpendicular bisector of the imaginary line QR.

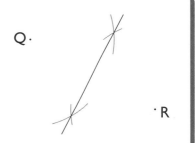

Overlapping regions

Example

Two amateur radio stations are situated at points A and B. Station A can pick up signals up to 4 km away and station B can pick up signals up to 2 km away. A ship in distress sends out signals which are picked up at both A and B. Show the region where the ship could be.

The area shaded ▧ shows the region where the ship could be.

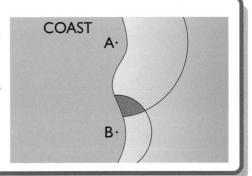

Exercise 2

A garden is 50 m by 30 m. Draw suitable lines to illustrate the information given.
- A patio 10 m wide is to be built adjoining the house. (see the line AD.)
- A seat is to be placed in the garden, far enough away from the fountain at F to avoid the spray, which can reach up to 7.5 m. Shade the region where the seat should not be placed.
- A tree is equidistant from both ends of the patio, and from BC and CD. Mark its position.

Leave all your construction lines on the diagram.

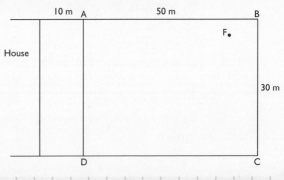

39

Distance, speed and time

Example

The diagram shows Mrs Brown's journey from home to her cousin's house and back. From the information given on the graph, answer the following questions.

a   How far away is her cousin's house?
b   Mrs Brown stopped after an hour to do some shopping. How far had she gone?
c   How long did she stay at her cousin's house?
d   How long did the journey home take?

Reading from the graph:
a   120 km
b   40 km
c $1\frac{1}{2}$ hours
d   2 hours

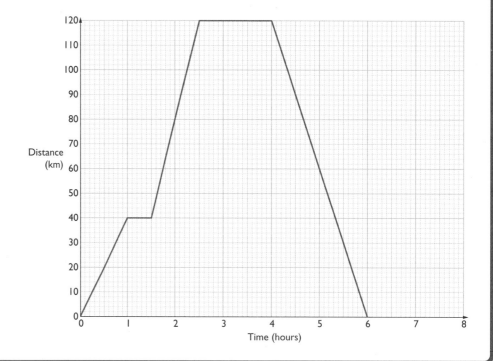

Exercise 1

Add the following information to the travel graph above.

1   Mrs Brown's daughter set off half an hour later and drove 50 km in the first 30 minutes of her journey.
2   It took her an hour to cover the remaining 70 km.
3   She stayed at the house for an hour before setting off for home. When she was halfway home, the car broke down and it was three hours before she could resume her journey. She drove at the same speed as her mother.
4   She kept driving at the same speed and finally arrived home two hours after her mother.

How to work out distance, speed and time questions without drawing a graph

Understanding the jargon

km/h kilometres per hour, the number of kilometres covered in 1 hour

Distance = speed × time   **Time = $\dfrac{\text{distance}}{\text{speed}}$**   **Speed = $\dfrac{\text{distance}}{\text{time}}$**

Example
Mrs Brown drove home
for 2 hours at 60 km/h.
She drove 2 × 60
= 120 km.

Example
Mrs Brown drove 120 km
at an average speed of
60 km/h. How long did the
journey take?
It took her 120 ÷ 60
= 2 hours.

Example
Mrs Brown drove 120 km
in 2 hours. What was her
speed in kilometres per
hour?
Her speed was 120 ÷ 2
= 60 km/h.

Example
A car travelled 560 km in 5 hours. What was the average speed in km/h?
Replace the per with ÷ and keep the figures in the same order.

km	per	hour	
560	÷	5	= 112 km/h

Be very careful to use the right units. If the question is worded in minutes, but the answer
requires hours, you must convert minutes to hours using fractions or decimals.

Exercise 2

1 A car travelled at an average speed of 100 km/h for
   3 hours.
   How far did it travel?
2 A car travelled 225 km at an average speed of
   90 km/h.
   How long did the journey take? Give your answer
   in hours and minutes.
3 A car went 340 km in three hours fifteen minutes.
   What was its average speed in km/hour?

Tactics

Whenever you see the
word 'per',
replace it with ÷.

Don't be stuPID.
Per Is Divide.

**Remember, 3.25 hours is 3 hours 15 minutes,
not 3 hours 25 minutes.**

RED ALERT

Area and perimeter

The area of a trapezium

A trapezium is a quadrilateral with one pair of parallel sides.
It may or may not be symmetrical.

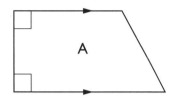 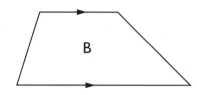 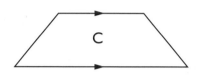

Example

Find the area of trapezium A below.

Solution 1
Split up the shape.

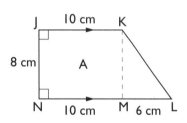

Area of rectangle JKMN = $10 \times 8 = 80$ cm^2
Area of triangle KML = $\frac{1}{2} \times 8 \times 6 = 24$ cm^2
Area of trapezium A = $80 + 24 = 104$ cm^2

Solution 2

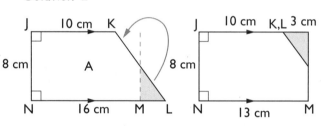

Cut a triangle from one corner as shown and
make a rectangle 13 cm $\times$ 8 cm.
Area = $8 \times 13 = 104$ cm^2

Exercise 1

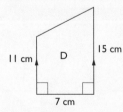 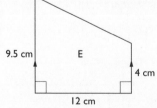 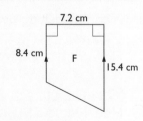

Choose whichever method you prefer to find the area of the trapezia D, E and F.

1 The area of trapezium D is _____ .
2 The area of trapezium E is _____ .
3 The area of trapezium F is _____ .

The formula for the area of a trapezium

Solution 1 works very well when the trapezium
has a pair of perpendicular sides, but it is not
as easy for a trapezium like B or C on page 42.

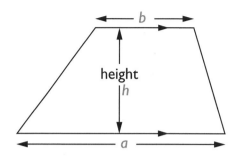

$$\text{Area} = \frac{a + b}{2} \times h$$

Example

The diagram shows a trapezium QRST (not
drawn to scale). RX is perpendicular to TS.
Find the area of the trapezium.

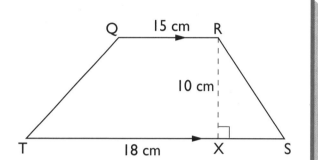

Use the formula

$$A = \frac{a + b}{2} \times h$$

with $a = 18$ cm

$b = 15$ cm and $h = 10$ cm.

$$\text{Area} = \frac{18 + 15}{2} \times 10 = 165 \text{ cm}^2$$

Exercise 2

Use the formula to work out the area of each trapezium.
All measurements are in centimetres.

	a	b	h
1	10	12	7
2	6.8	10.3	5.4
3	24	27	14

Solving area and perimeter problems

Example
Write an expression for the perimeter of this rectangle.

The perimeter is the distance all the way round the shape, so one expression is $15 + a + 15 + a$.
This simplifies to $30 + 2a$ cm.
You can also work out the perimeter by adding a length and a width and then doubling, so another formula could be $(15 + a) \times 2$ or $2(15 + a)$ cm, which can also be rewritten as $30 + 2a$ cm.
The area is $15a$ cm^2.

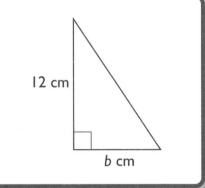

15 cm

a cm

Example
Write an expression for the area of this triangle.
The area is $12b \div 2 = 6b$ cm^2.

You can also use the formula
$A = \frac{1}{2}$ base $\times$ height

to give $\frac{1}{2} \times b \times 12$, which simplifies to $6b$ cm^2.

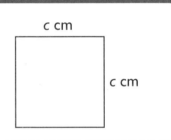

12 cm

b cm

Example
a   Write an expression for the perimeter of this square.
b   Write an expression for the area of the square.

a   The perimeter is $c + c + c + c = 4c$ cm.
b   The area is c^2 cm^2.

c cm

c cm

Exercise 3

1   A square has sides s cm long.
   a   What is its area?
   b   What is its perimeter?
   c   A diagonal line splits the square into two triangles.
     What is the area of each triangle?

2   **a**   The area of a square is t^2 cm^2.
     What is the length of each side?
   b   The perimeter of a rectangle is $14 + 8v$ cm.
     If the length is 7 cm, find the width in terms of v.

Tactics

You can sometimes spot perpendicular lines by looking for right angles marked on the diagram.

RED ALERT!   To find areas of rectangles and triangles you must multiply lengths that are perpendicular.   **RED**

Example

David and Lindsay each draw the same rectangle.
The perimeter of David's rectangle is $5n + 3$ cm.
The perimeter of Lindsay's rectangle is $2n + 15$ cm.

Find the value of n and the perimeter of the rectangles.
Since the rectangles are the same, the perimeters must be equal.

$$5n + 3 = 2n + 15$$
$$3n = 12$$
$$n = 4$$

The perimeter of the rectangle is 23 cm.

Example

Gina and Adam have drawn rectangles. The ratio of the sides of Gina's rectangle to the sides of Adam's rectangle is 2 : 1.

a If Gina's rectangle is w cm long, how long is Adam's?
b If Adam's rectangle is z cm wide, how wide is Gina's?

a Gina's rectangle is twice as long as Adam's, so Adam's must be half the length of Gina's.
The length of Adam's rectangle is $\frac{1}{2}w$ or $\frac{w}{2}$.
b Gina's rectangle is twice as wide as Adam's, so its width is $2z$.

Exercise 4

A rectangle measuring 12 cm by n cm is
cut into three equal strips, as shown.

1 What is the area of piece J ?
2 What is the perimeter of the rectangle
formed by J and K?
3 J, K and L are rearranged to make a
vertical column.

    a What are the height and width of the column?
    b What is the perimeter?
    c What is the area?

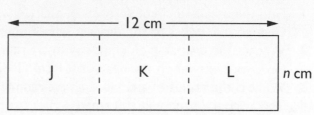

Be careful to write squared units for area.   RED ALERT

Circles

184 cm² (handwritten)

> **Example**
>
> A circle has a radius of 5.7 cm. Find its area and its circumference.
> Area of a circle = $\pi r^2 = \pi \times 5.7^2 = 102$ cm² correct to 3 s.f.
> Radius = 5.7 cm so diameter = 5.7 × 2 = 11.4 cm
> Circumference of a circle = πd = 11.4 × π = 35.8 cm

39.78   125 m (handwritten)

How to find the diameter if you know the circumference

This is easy if you approximate π to 3. $C = 3d$, so $C \div 3 = d$
$C = \pi \times d$ so the diameter is the circumference divided by π. $d = C \div \pi$.

Solving circle questions

Memorise the formulae for the area and the circumference of a circle.
Area of a circle = πr^2 (πr squarea gives you the area.) Circumference = πd or $2\pi r$.
Always write down your working. Use the $\boxed{\pi}$ key on your calculator.
You may need to use $\boxed{\text{inv}}$, $\boxed{\text{shift}}$ or $\boxed{\text{2nd F}}$.

> **Example**
>
> A circle and square have the same area when rounded to 2 s.f. The radius of the circle is 4.5 cm
> What is the length of one of the sides of the square?
>
> The area of the circle is $\pi \times 4.5^2 = 63.6 = 64$ cm² to 2 s.f.
> Each side of the square = $\sqrt{64} = 8$ cm.

> **Example**
>
> Work out the circumference of the circle and the perimeter of the square in the last
> example. Round your answers to the nearest cm. What is the ratio of the circumference of
> the circle to the perimeter of the square? Give your answer in its simplest form.
> Radius of the circle = 4.5 cm. Diameter = 9 cm
> Circumference = $\pi \times d = \pi \times 9 = 28$ cm. Perimeter of the square = 4 × 8 = 32 cm
> Ratio circumference of circle : perimeter of square = 28 : 32 = 7 : 8.

Exercise 1

1   Find the area and circumference of a circle with diameter 26.8 cm.
    Give your answers to the nearest whole number.
2   What is the diameter of a circle with a circumference of 40 cm?
    Give your answer to the nearest 0.1 cm (1 d.p.).
3   What is the radius of a circle with a circumference of 100 cm?
4   The area of a square is 100 cm².
    a   Find the length of one of the sides.
    b   Find the radius and area of the largest circle that would fit inside it.
    c   What percentage of the square would not be covered by the circle?
5   A circle has a circumference of 96 cm to the nearest cm.
    a   Find its radius.   b   Use your answer to **a** to find the area of its semicircle.

Circumference, distance and turns

> **Example**
>
> A wheel on a cart has a radius of 35 cm. How many complete turns does it make when the cart travels 50 m?
> First, find the circumference.
> Circumference = π × 70 = 219.91 cm
> Distance travelled = 5000 cm
>
> $\dfrac{\text{Distance}}{\text{Circumference}}$ = Turns $\dfrac{5000}{219.91}$ = 22.7 = 22 complete turns.

Turns are sometimes called revolutions.

Approximating answers

Often, a rough answer or approximation is enough. In any case, since π goes on for ever, we cannot usually give a complete and totally accurate answer when using it.

If you are not sure how far to round a number, round it to the least accurate number given in the question. This is the measurement with the smallest number of significant figures or places of decimals.

> **Example**
>
> The girth (circumference) of a tree is measured as 250 cm. What is its diameter?
> Diameter = circumference ÷ π = 250 ÷ π = 79.577 471 545 9...
> The circumference is given to 2 s.f.
> Diameter = 80 cm correct to 2 s.f.

> **Example**
>
> The diameter of the Earth is approximately 12 900 km. What is the approximate length of the equator?
> The equator is a circle with a diameter of 12 900 km.
> C = π × 12 900 = 40 526.545 231 3...
> The diameter is given to 3 s.f.
> Circumference = 40 500 km correct to 3 s.f.

Exercise 2

1 A wheel on a cart has a diameter of 1.5 m. How far does the cart travel when the wheel makes 20 revolutions?

2 The diameter of a bicycle wheel is 65 cm. How many complete turns does it make in travelling 1 km?

3 A tin has a diameter of 10.5 cm. A label is put round the tin. How long is the label if it just fits, with no overlap?

4 Surveyors use an odometer to measure distances along the ground. It goes round once for every metre the odometer is pushed. What is the diameter of the odometer? Give your answer in centimetres correct to 1 d.p.

Tactics

How to remember the formula
Send for the DoCTor.
Distance = Circumference × Turns

$\dfrac{\text{Distance}}{\text{Circumference}}$ = Turns

$\dfrac{\text{Distance}}{\text{Turns}}$ = Circumference

Volume

Understanding the jargon

Cube   a 3D shape with six square faces
Cuboid   a 3D shape with six rectangular faces, opposite faces are equal
Volume   the amount of space taken up by a 3D object
Capacity   the amount of space inside a hollow 3D container

The volume of a cuboid

Volume = length × width × height
Area is measured in square units.
Volume is measured in cubic units.

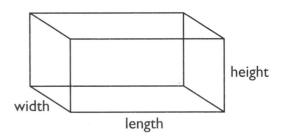

Example
The dimensions of a box are 30 cm, 25 cm and 10 cm. Find the volume of the box.
Volume = 30 × 25 × 10 = 7500 cm^3

Calculators and cubed numbers

Example
A cube has sides of length 45 cm. Find the volume of the cube.
The slow way is to work out 45 × 45 × 45.
Calculators have a $\boxed{y^x}$ or $\boxed{x^y}$ key which is very useful, particularly if the number you are cubing has several digits.
Many calculators work like this
45^3 = 45 $\boxed{y^x}$ or $\boxed{x^y}$ 3 = 91125
Volume = 91 125 cm^3

Exercise 1

1   How many centimetre cubes could you fit into a box measuring 30 cm by 12 cm by 3 cm?

2   **a**   Find the volume of a cube with sides of length 7.5 cm. Write down all the numbers on your calculator display.

    b   Round your answer to part **a** to 3 s.f.

The volume of a cylinder

Volume = area of base × height
The base of a cylinder is a circle.
You will sometimes see the formula for the volume (V) of a cylinder
written as:
$V = \pi r^2 h$

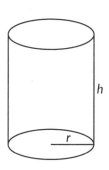

Example
A cylinder has a radius of 5 cm and a height of 20 cm. Find its volume.
Area of the base = πr^2
$\qquad\qquad\quad = \pi \times 5^2$
$\qquad\qquad\quad = 78.54$ cm^2
Volume = area × height
$\qquad\quad = 78.54 \times 20$
$\qquad\quad = 1571$ cm^3

Capacity

The capacity of a container is usually a liquid measure.
You measure liquids using litres (l) and millilitres (ml).
1 millilitre = 1 cm^3
1 litre = 1000 cm^3

Example
A cylindrical container has a base area of 240 cm^2 and a height of 30 cm. How many litres
does it hold?
Volume = 240×30
$\qquad\quad = 7200$ cm^3
7200 cm^3 = 7.2 litres

Exercise 2

1 Find the volume of a cylinder with radius 3.5 cm and
   height 15 cm.
2 a A cylinder has radius 20 cm and height 40 cm.
       Find its volume, in litres.
   b How many glasses of liquid each holding 200 ml
      could be filled from it? (Remember to use either ml
      or litres, so you work in the same unit of measurement.)

Tactics

You can change cubic
centimetres to litres
by dividing by 1000.

ERT RED ALERT RED ALERT! RED ALERT RED ALERT

The volume of a prism

Understanding the jargon

Prism   a 3D shape that can be cut into identical slices
Cross-section   face of a prism cut perpendicular to its length

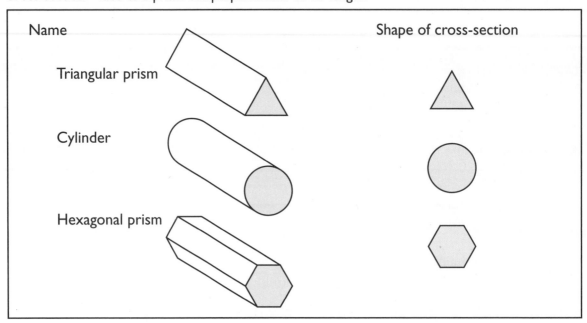

Name	Shape of cross-section
Triangular prism	
Cylinder	
Hexagonal prism	

Volume of a prism = area of cross-section × height (or length) of the prism

Example

The diagram, not drawn to scale, shows a triangular prism of length 15 cm. The cross-section is a triangle with base 8 cm and height 5 cm. Find the volume of the prism.

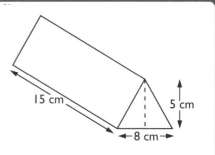

Volume = area of cross-section × 15

Area of triangle = $\frac{1}{2}(8 \times 5) = 20$ cm^2

Volume = $15 \times 20 = 300$ cm^3

Exercise 3

1 Find the volume of a triangular prism of length 30 cm, with a triangular cross-section of base 6 cm and height 8.5 cm.

2 A hexagonal box has a base area of 56 cm^2 and its height is 25 cm. Find the volume of the box.

Tactics

When you cut a prism at right angles to its length, the slice is a cross-section of the prism. It will be the same shape wherever you cut the prism along its length.

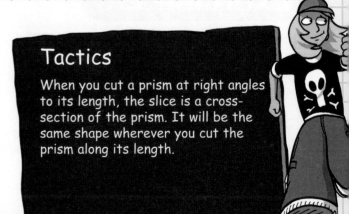

50

Some prisms aren't so obvious.

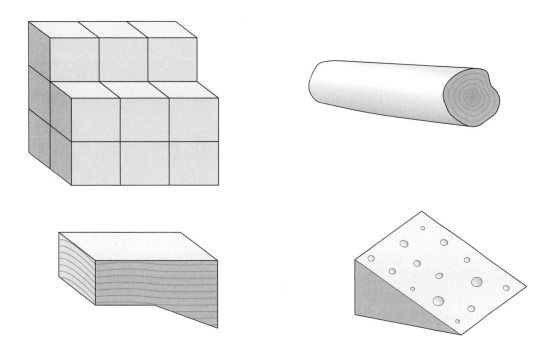

Sometimes the container can't be completely filled.

> **Example**
> A box is 25 cm long, 20 cm wide and 7 cm high. What is the maximum number of 2 cm cubes
> which will fit in the box so that the lid will shut?
> You could fit 12 along the length, 10 along the width and have 3 layers.
> The maximum number is $12 \times 10 \times 3 = 360$ cubes

Exercise 4

1 Using the same dimensions as in the example above, how many 3 cm cubes would fit
   with the lid still being able to shut?
2 A cuboid has a volume of 1200 cm³. If the length is 20 cm and the width is 10 cm,
   find the height.

4

How to revise maths

You can revise some subjects by reading a text, but maths doesn't work like that. The only way to be sure that you can do maths is by doing maths!

- Start your revision by deciding which topics you need to study. If you are working towards an end-of-year exam, or a National Test, your teacher may give you a revision list. If you don't have any guidance, look back through your old exercise books, or worksheets that you have done, and list the topics that are there. Find them on the Number network in this book and see if you need to backtrack and brush up on some skills before you get started. Finding the topic on the network will show you other related topics where you will need this knowledge, and may encourage you to keep going when you realise that perhaps you know more than you think.

- With the order settled, you can get down to some serious revision. Look over a worked example on your first topic and see if you can follow the reasoning. If you think that you understand, cover up the example, leaving only the top line visible. Then work through the example, line by line, trying to predict what is coming next. Write down your working and compare it, a line at a time, with the worked example. Try to work out the next line of the answer each time before you uncover it.

- When you feel confident, try an example yourself. If the answer is correct, try a few more to make certain that it wasn't just a lucky guess and then, if possible, try some more complicated examples.

- You will probably find some topics easier than others. Try the 'little and often' rule for those areas that cause you problems. Don't worry if you can't master something at the first or second attempt. Get part way through a process and concentrate on being able to do that. Simultaneous equations, for instance, are complicated, so concentrate on getting the first part right - getting the same number of either x or y (or whatever letters are used in the question) in both equations. Try it with different questions until you are sure about it. Then go on to the next part - adding or subtracting the equations.

- If you break a complicated process down into smaller steps and practise each skill until you are really confident, you shouldn't find that awful panic setting in as you frantically try to remember what comes next.

- Your teacher or school may insist that you use a particular method, but sometimes you may find another way of tackling a problem – one that perhaps makes better sense to you. Often teachers will accept a different way of doing things as long as it's based on sound mathematical reasoning and doesn't ramble on for six pages. If you do find a way that you prefer and can show your teacher how well you can make it work, you may be allowed to use it and, who knows, you may just be able to teach your teacher something!

- When you are revising, remember that you will probably have to face some exams when you may use a calculator and others where a calculator is not allowed. For the non-calculator paper, try to give yourself some practice in advance. You can quietly practise mental arithmetic by totting up the cost of a few items, and the change that you should receive, whilst waiting to pay for a magazine or a pizza. Nobody needs to know that you are doing it – or even whether you get it right.

- If possible, don't rely on a calculator to do processes that you are perfectly capable of carrying out yourself and which will probably come up on a non–calculator paper. Long multiplication, division and percentages are almost always lurking on a non–calculator paper somewhere, whereas even the most hardhearted examiner will probably not expect you to work out circle questions or use Pythagoras' theorem without a calculator.

- A calculator is very efficient at carrying out the most complicated calculations in a fraction of the time it would take most of us to do them using mere brains but it can only do as it is told. Garbage in definitely produces garbage out, so you need to know that you are giving it the right instruction. Remember, by now you should be working with a scientific calculator, so BoDMAS rules, okay?

A LARGE PEPPERONI IS £7·80... PLUS GARLIC BREAD AT £1·85... MAKES £9·65, GIVING ME 35p CHANGE FROM A TEN POUND NOTE!

Questions and answers

Understanding the jargon

Hypothesis   an idea, often put forward as a possible explanation for an event
Sample   a group of people selected from the whole available population (For instance, instead of asking every pupil in the school their views on school uniform, you just ask a sample of 10% of pupils.)
Survey   questions, often in a questionnaire, designed to find out the views of people in the sample

Examples

- The pupils who ran the school tuck shop noticed that their sales of crisps had gone down. A new supermarket had opened near the school that month.
  Hypothesis: *Pupils who used to buy crisps from the school tuck shop are now buying their crisps from the supermarket instead.*
- Local shopkeepers wanted to find ways of increasing their trade.
  Hypothesis: *More customers would shop in the evening if the shops stayed open later.*

Asking the questions

You must be very careful to get the respondents' views and opinions without trying to influence them. For example, in the tuck shop situation, you could ask:
- Have you bought crisps this week   ❑ yes   ❑ no
- If yes, where did you buy them?   ❑ tuck shop   ❑ supermarket   ❑ other
- If you didn't buy them from the tuck shop, was the reason:
    ❑ tuck shop crisps cost more   ❑ the supermarket is more convenient   ❑ other?

Do not ask:
- Do you usually buy crisps from the tuck shop?
  This is too vague – how usual is 'usually'? Maybe your respondent *never* buys crisps.
- Don't you agree that we should support the tuck shop?
  This is a leading question – you are encouraging respondents to answer in a certain way.

Exercise 1

1 What is a possible hypothesis for a bus company thinking about starting a new bus route?
2 A country cinema is considering putting on a coach service to encourage more people to visit at night. Write a hypothesis that they could use.

Tactics

Choose a sample to represent all those who are involved. In the question involving the tuck shop, pupils should be chosen from all those affected, not just one year group or form.

RED ALERT!   **Avoid bias – testing a hypothesis is only useful if the results are unbiased.**   RED

Recording data

It is easier to understand and use data recorded in a visual way, such as in:
*   bar charts
*   pictograms
*   pie charts.

Suppose a manufacturer of crisps wanted to test some possible new products, and invited a group of a hundred children to take part in a tasting session, and then gave them a questionnaire to fill in.

The results could have been recorded like this.

Favourite flavours	%
salt and vinegar	25%
ready salted	23%
cheese and onion	35%
prawn cocktail	10%
bacon	5%
beef and onion	2%

Although it is presented in a table, the information does not show the differences very clearly. A chart or diagram has more impact.

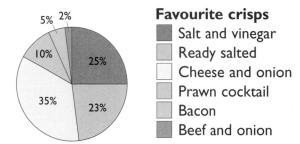

Favourite crisps
- Salt and vinegar
- Ready salted
- Cheese and onion
- Prawn cocktail
- Bacon
- Beef and onion

Comparing data

It is often very useful to be able to compare data from two different samples.

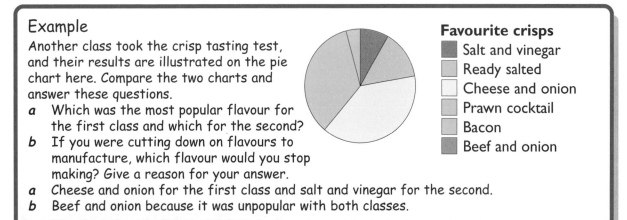

Example
Another class took the crisp tasting test, and their results are illustrated on the pie chart here. Compare the two charts and answer these questions.
a Which was the most popular flavour for the first class and which for the second?
b If you were cutting down on flavours to manufacture, which flavour would you stop making? Give a reason for your answer.

Favourite crisps
- Salt and vinegar
- Ready salted
- Cheese and onion
- Prawn cocktail
- Bacon
- Beef and onion

a Cheese and onion for the first class and salt and vinegar for the second.
b Beef and onion because it was unpopular with both classes.

Exercise 2

1 Draw a bar chart for the data in the top pie chart. Put the categories on the horizontal axes and the percentages on the vertical axes. Which do you think shows the information more clearly, your bar chart or the table?

2 Pupils were asked where they would like to live. Rounded to the nearest 5%, their views were as follows. Draw a bar chart to show these figures.
   city centre 20% suburb 15% seaside 50% countryside 15%

3 Work out the sizes of angle necessary to represent this data on a pie chart.
   city centre 20% suburb 15% seaside 50% countryside 15%

Scatter graphs

Understanding the jargon

Correlation   relationship between two or more events. For example, a café might find that more ice creams are sold during hot weather. The warmer the weather, the more ice creams are sold. This is positive correlation. Both factors increase or decrease together. As the temperature goes up, though, less soup will probably be called for. This is negative correlation. As one factor, i.e. temperature, increases the other factor, i.e. sales of soup, decreases. If no relationship can be found, then there is no correlation.

Scatter graphs   sometimes called scatter diagrams, a way of showing whether or not two sets of data correlate

Example

A set of students took two tests, one in French and one in English.
Their results are given below.

French	17	13	7	18	12	20	15	8	10
English	30	21	12	35	19	38	20	10	18

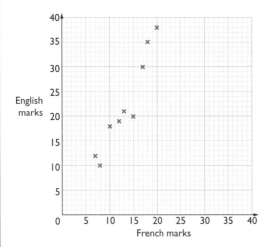

It is difficult to learn anything about the group from the raw scores, so they are plotted on a scatter graph.
The points go upwards fairly steadily and this shows positive correlation.
The same students were tested in physics, and also entered for the school high jump competition.
There was no correlation found. Ability to jump well does not appear to relate to a student's ability in physics.

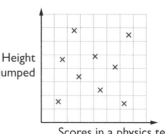

Scores in a physics test

Exercise 1

1 It was found that young children's vocabulary increased with age. Which graph would you expect shows this?

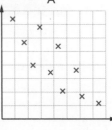
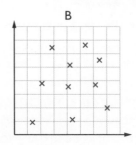
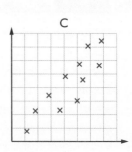

A   B   C

2 What kind of correlation would you call this relationship?
3 Which graph shows negative correlation?
4 Which graph shows no correlation?

Line of best fit

To make the graphs easier to read, and to use them to interpret other data, draw a line through as many points as possible. There should be as many points above the line as below it. This is the line of best fit.

Example

Add a line of best fit to the scatter diagram from page 56. Use the diagram to answer the following questions.

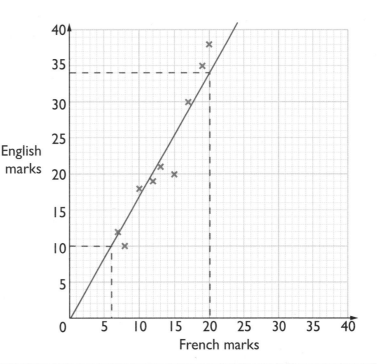

a Emma was away for the English test but scored 20 in the French test. What mark might she have scored in English?

b Anthony was away for the French test but scored 10 in the English test. What mark might he have scored in French?

Either draw lines as shown or read off the values.

a Emma's mark in French would probably have been 34.

b Anthony's mark in English would probably have been 6.

Exercise 2

An experiment was held to see whether students improved at performing a task if they trained first. The results were plotted on a graph, and a line of best fit was drawn. Use the graph to answer these questions.

1 What kind of correlation does the graph show?

2 A student completed the task in 10 minutes. For how long is he likely to have trained?

3 One student's result has been wrongly plotted. According to the graph, how long did that student train and what were her results?

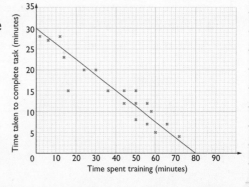

Averages and range

Understanding the jargon

Mean   the total of all the values divided by the number of values
Median   the middle value when the values have been arranged in order, smallest to largest
Mode the most common value (There can be more than one mode.)
Range   the difference between the largest value and the smallest value

Averages

> ### Example
> a   Find the mean, median, mode and range of the following set of numbers.
>   3, 7, 2, 8, 8, 1, 8, 4, 6, 5
> b   The mean value of this set of cards is $4x$, but one of these cards has been turned over.
>   What is written on the other side of that card?
>
>
>
> a $3 + 7 + 2 + 8 + 8 + 1 + 8 + 4 + 7 + 4 = 52$
>   • The mean $= 52 \div 10 = 5.2$
>   • The median value is halfway between the fifth and sixth values, when they are placed
>   in order. The fifth value is 4 and the sixth value is 7. The median is 5.5.
>   • The most frequent value is 8, so 8 is the mode.
>   • The range is $8 - 1 = 7$
> b   The total must be the equivalent of $4x + 4x + 4x = 12x$. The third card must be $4x - 5$.
>   *Check*: $4x + 4x + 5 + 4x - 5 = 12x$

Exercise 1

1   Find the mean, median, mode and range of the following set of numbers.
   3.9, 4.1, 2.7, 2.7, 5.6
2   What is the mean value of these two cards?

Working backwards

Example

a   The mean of these cards is 4. What number is on the reverse of the card?

b   The mode of these cards is 3. What number is on the reverse of the card?

c   The median of these cards is 10. What number is on the reverse of the card?

a   The mean is 4, so the total is $5 \times 4 = 20$. The total on the four cards showing is 19, so the missing number is 1.

b   You need another 3 so that 3 appears twice and the other numbers appear once.

c   10

Mean, median and mode are all averages, but when people talk about averages they are usually referring to the mean.

Exercise 2

1   The range of these cards is 5. What is the missing number?

2   The mean of these cards is 12, What is the missing number?

3   The median of these cards is 10. What is the missing number?

Finding the mean – a quicker way for large numbers

Example

Class 9W was carrying out research into local car use. As part of the research they investigated the mean number of people per car to travel past the school at different times of the day.

Here is their result for 10 – 11 a.m. one Monday morning.

Number of people	1	2	3	4	5
Number of cars	30	35	20	5	1

Find the mean number of people per car.

If there were 30 cars each carrying one person, there would be 30 people altogether.

If there were 35 cars each carrying two people, there would be 70 people altogether.

Total number of people $= 1 \times 30 + 2 \times 35 + 3 \times 20 + 4 \times 5 + 1 \times 5 = 185$

Total number of cars $= 30 + 35 + 20 + 5 + 1 = 91$

Mean number of people per car $= \dfrac{\text{total number of people}}{\text{total number of cars}} = \dfrac{185}{91} = 2.0$ (to 2 s.f.)

Exercise 3

In a recent sponsored swim, an upper limit of £5 per student was put on the collection. One class collected the following amounts of money.

Amount (£)	1	2	3	4	5
Number of students	1	3	7	12	12

1   What was the total amount collected?

2   What was the mean amount collected per student?

3   What was the modal amount collected?

RED ALERT!   **To find the total number of people, you need to multiply and not simply add 1 + 2 + 3 + 4 + 5. In the mean time, times for the mean.**   **RED**

Grouped data

Sometimes the data is not given as a set of individual figures, but is grouped.

Example

Class 9W collected ring pulls to sell for charity.
The numbers they collected were grouped as follows.

Number of ring pulls	Number of students
10-20	4
21-30	10
31-40	15
41-50	1

a Find the mean number of ring pulls collected.
b What was the modal group?

As the question does not give an exact figure for each student, take a midpoint. In the group 10–20, for instance, the maximum number of ring pulls collected would have been 20 and the lowest number would have been 10. Assume that the students collected the middle amount, called the mid-interval value, i.e. 15, and say that the group collected $4 \times 15 = 60$. This allows for some to have done better than that and some to have done worse.
The table looks like this:

Number of ring pulls	Number of students	Mid-interval value	Total
10-20	4	15	$4 \times 15 = 60$
21-30	10	25.5	$10 \times 25.5 = 255$
31-40	15	35.5	$15 \times 35.5 = 532.5$
41-50	1	45.5	$1 \times 45.5 = 45.5$
		Total =	$60 + 255 + 532.5 + 45.5 = 893$

a Mean number of ring pulls per student = $893 \div 30 = 29.8$
   The mean was 30 ring pulls.
b The modal group is the group to which most students belong.
   It is 31-40, so 31–40 is the modal group.

Exercise 4

A teacher recorded the marks gained in a recent test as follows.

Marks gained	Number of students
0–5	3
6–10	14
11–15	10
16–20	3

Find:

1 the mid-interval values   2 the modal group   3 the mean number of marks gained.

Frequency polygons

Brushing up on bar charts

The information about the marks gained by the students in the last exercise could be displayed on a bar chart.

It could also be shown on a frequency polygon.

To draw a frequency polygon, start by thinking of a bar chart. Mark just the midpoint of the top of each bar, and then join up the points with straight lines.

This frequency polygon below shows the same information as the bar chart above it.

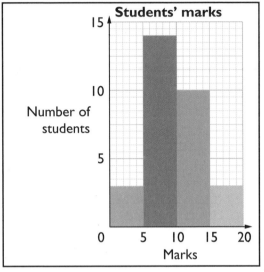

Sometimes you will see frequency polygons drawn with the lines going down to the horizontal axis, and sometimes not, as shown here. Ask your teacher which you should do.

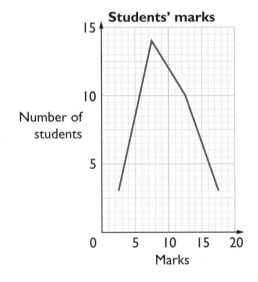

Exercise 1

A class was timed solving a maths problem, and the results were recorded to the nearest minute. The data was then grouped as shown below.

Time taken (minutes)	Number of pupils
1–5	2
6–10	14
11–15	10
16–20	4

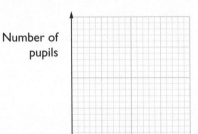

1   Draw a bar chart to show this information.
2   Draw a frequency polygon to show this information.

RED ALERT!   **Join the points on the frequency polygon with straight lines.**   RED

Interpreting frequency polygons

Example

The frequency polygon shows the results of a test completed by year 9 students at Hunt's High School. Use the graph to answer these questions.

a   What was the modal group?

b   How many pupils scored between 80 and 90 marks?

c   Between what marks was the lowest score?

a   20–30

b   5 pupils

c   10–20

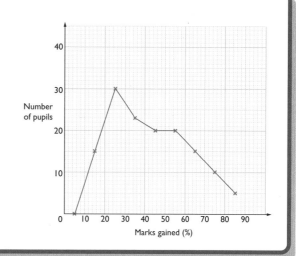

You can also use frequency polygons to compare scores.

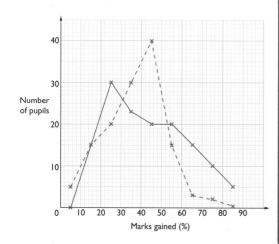

Example

The same test was given to another year 9 group at Chute School.

Using the frequency polygon diagram, answer the following questions.

a   What was the modal group for Chute School?

b   How many pupils scored between 50 and 60 marks?

c   Which school do you think performed better? Give a reason for your answer.

a   40–50

b   15 pupils

c   You could say either group. Group 1 had more students with very high marks than group 2. Group 2 had a higher mode and fewer students with very low marks. It does not matter which you choose as long as you have a good reason.

Exercise 2

People were asked to guess the weight of a parcel. The results were divided into categories – up to but not including 250 g, between 250 g and up to but not including 500 g and so on. The frequency polygon shows the results.

1   Which was the modal group?

2   If the group choosing the lowest weight and the group choosing the highest weight changed their minds and thought that the weight was between 1 kg and 1.25 kg, what would be the modal group? Give a reason for your answer.

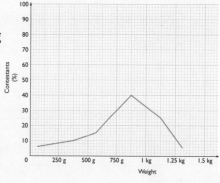

Probability

Basic revision

Some things in life are certain.
- If today is Monday, tomorrow will be Tuesday.
- If today is Monday, tomorrow cannot be Friday.

Most things in life, though, are not 100% certain to happen or not to happen. The likelihood or not of an event occurring is its probability.

Example
For each of the following events, say whether it is:

impossible   unlikely   fifty-fifty   likely   certain

a   If today is Saturday, tomorrow will be Sunday.
b   It will snow at least once in July in London.
c   It will rain at least once in January in London.
d   If you toss a coin it will land heads up.

a   certain
b   unlikely
c   likely
d   fifty-fifty

Exercise 1

Choose one of these options above to answer the following questions.

impossible   unlikely   fifty-fifty   likely   certain

1   There are 100 pence in a pound.
2   April will follow May this year.
3   In an all boys' school, the next person you meet on the stairs will be male.
4   If a bag contains exactly 40 marbles, all of which are either red or green, and the chances of choosing either colour are fifty-fifty, what does this tell you about the number of red and the number of green marbles in the bag?

Measuring probability

It is usual to measure probability more precisely than just as 'likely' or 'fifty-fifty'.
You can use fractions, decimals or percentages but not ratios.
Instead of saying that Neil had a one in four chance of choosing a yellow sweet from a packet of mixed sweets, you would say that his chance of picking a yellow sweet is $\frac{1}{4}$ or 0.25 or 25%.
Measure probability using fractions, decimals or percentages as:

number of outcomes that give desired result
total number of possible outcomes

The probabilities of all the possible outcomes of an event add up to exactly 1.

Example
There are 52 playing cards in an ordinary pack. 13 of them are hearts.
a What is the probability of drawing a heart from a full pack?
b What is the probability of not drawing a heart from a full pack?

a 13 out of 52 = $\frac{13}{52}$ = $\frac{1}{4}$ or 0.25 or 25%

b If $\frac{1}{4}$ are hearts, $\frac{3}{4}$ or 0.75 or 75% are not hearts. The probability of not drawing a heart

is $\frac{3}{4}$ or 0.75 or 75%.

Example
In this row of cards, there are more cards with stars than with crosses. What could be on the other side of the two hidden cards – stars or crosses?

There could be two stars or one star and one cross.

Exercise 2

A pack contains cards with either stars or crosses on the front. Eight cards are placed face down and three of them turned over, as shown.

What would be on the front of the other cards, if:
1 the probability that the card has a cross on it is 0.5
2 the probability that the card has a cross on it is 0
3 the probability that the card has a star on it is $\frac{3}{4}$?

Relative frequency

If you have worked out the probability of an event happening, you can work out the effect of the probability by using its relative frequency.

Example

In a recent epidemic, 10 out of 25 members of a class caught 'flu.

a What was the probability of a class member catching 'flu?

b In a school of 600 pupils, how many would you expect to catch 'flu?

a 10 out of 25 $= \frac{10}{25} = \frac{2}{5}$

The probability of catching 'flu is $\frac{2}{5}$.

b In a school of 600 pupils, $\frac{2}{5}$ of 600 $= 600 \div 5 \times 2 = 240$.

It would be reasonable to expect 240 pupils to catch 'flu.

Exercise 3

1 The probability that the school football team wins a match is 0.8. If it plays 20 matches during the season, how many would you expect them to lose?

2 Out of 30 000 visitors to a town last season, 6000 visited the museum.
   a What is the probability that one visitor, stopped at random, visited the museum?
   b If the town hopes to attract 45 000 visitors this year, how many would you expect to visit the museum?

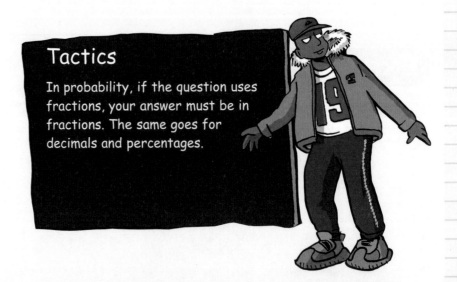

Tactics

In probability, if the question uses fractions, your answer must be in fractions. The same goes for decimals and percentages.

RED ALERT! RED   **Never use a ratio for a probability.**   ALERT RE

Fair or biased?

We can use relative frequency to spot bias – or cheating!

Example

a   Work out the probabilities of spinning 4, 5 or 6 if this spinner is fair.

b   If you spun the spinner 120 times, how many of each number would you expect to get?

c   Natalie said that in 120 spins she had scored 50 sixes. Do you think that she was telling the truth?

a   The probability of spinning a 4 is $\frac{3}{6} = \frac{1}{2}$.

The probability of spinning a 5 is $\frac{2}{6} = \frac{1}{3}$.

The probability of spinning a 6 is $\frac{1}{6}$.

b

Number	Number of times
4	60
5	40
6	20

c   It is unlikely, given the relative frequency – but you would have to know Natalie to be really convinced either way!

Exercise 4

A
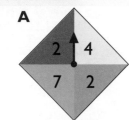

B
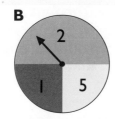

1 a   The two spinners are spun and the results are multiplied together. Set out a table, as drawn below, and work out all the possible pairs.

×	2	2	4	7
1				
2				
2				
5				

Notice that there are two entries for 2 on Spinner B. Look carefully at the diagram and see if you can work out why.

   b   What is the probability of scoring 4?
   c   What is the probability of scoring a multiple of 5?
   d   What is the probability of scoring less than 2?

2 If you spun the spinners 64 times, how many times would you expect to get a score of 4?

3 Louise said that you are more likely to get a 2 on spinner A than on spinner B, as there are more sections with a 2. Andrew said that she was wrong. Who was right, and why?

4 Rachel spun the spinners ten times. She said that on six attempts she scored 4, so the spinners weren't fair. Comment on her result.

5

Getting ready for the National Tests

Syllabus information

All state schools, and some independent schools too, sit National Tests (also known as SATS). In maths, you will take one calculator and one non-calculator paper, and a mental arithmetic test. The papers are usually set at levels 4–6, 5–7 or 6–8. The material overlaps so that, for instance, the same level 5 questions are used on 4–6 and 5–7 papers, but you won't find them on 6–8. All papers cover level 6, so the same level 6 questions are used on 4–6, 5–7 and 6–8. If you choose a higher level combination, you must know the earlier material, so here is a checklist for the main topics for each level. Although you may choose 4–6 for your national test, there is life after SATS and you will probably cover some level 7 material later in the summer term in year 9.

NB 'The four rules' are adding, subtracting, multiplying and dividing.

Levels 4 and 5

Number and algebra

I can:
- use the four rules of number, both with and without a calculator
- calculate using fractions, decimals and percentages
- add and subtract negative numbers
- recognise number patterns and sequences and work out their rules
- use single brackets in algebra
- use coordinates in all four quadrants.

Shape, space and measures

I can:
- find perimeters and areas of shapes by counting squares
- work out the area of a rectangle and a triangle by using a formula

- measure and draw angles to the nearest degree
- work with metric measures – cm, m, km, gram, kg, tonne
- change common imperial measures still in use to their approximate metric equivalents – pounds, ounces, inches, feet and yards.

Handling data

I can:
- work out the mean, median, mode and range of a set of data
- draw and answer questions using bar charts, line graphs, pictograms and pie charts
- solve probability questions.

● Level 6

Number and algebra

I can:
- round numbers using decimal places
- multiply and divide negative numbers
- use proportion and ratio
- find the nth term in a sequence where the difference between terms is the same and does not involve n^2
- formulate and solve simple equations (those involving one letter, called a variable, at a time. The variable isn't squared or cubed.)
- calculate one number as a fraction or percentage of another
- draw graphs using all four quadrants
- use mappings.

● Shape, space and measures

I can:
- recognise the plan view and front and side elevation of shapes
- use reflections, rotations, translations and enlargements
- recognise when shapes tessellate and work out the angles of polygons
- find the volume of a cube or cuboid
- find the area and circumference of a circle using π
- use computer instructions to draw shapes.

Handling data

I can:
- collect and record data using class intervals
- use scatter diagrams
- use diagrams and two-way tables to calculate probability.

Level 7

Number and algebra

I can:
- round numbers using significant figures
- solve simultaneous equations using algebra or graphs
- multiply and simplify expressions using double brackets
- find the nth term in a sequence involving n^2.

Shape, space and measures

I can:
- use Pythagoras' theorem
- enlarge shapes by a fractional scale factor
- work out loci questions
- solve distance, speed and time questions.

Handling data

I can:
- work out the modal class, the mean, median and mode of grouped data
- draw a line of best fit on a scatter diagram
- draw and answer questions using frequency polygons
- understand and calculate relative frequency.

Level 8

Level 8 material isn't covered in this book, but here is the checklist.

Number and algebra

I can:
- use standard form
- use fractions, decimals, percentages to solve equations
- rearrange algebraic formulae.

Shape, space and measures

I can:
- recognise congruent or similar shapes
- do trigonometry using right-angled triangles
- recognise a formula for length, area or volume by considering dimensions.

Handling data

I can:
- draw cumulative frequency diagrams
- solve probability questions using and/or.

How to tackle maths exams

Nowadays you usually have to try to answer all the questions on a maths exam, so there is no point wasting time reading through the whole paper first. Start at the beginning and just keep going.

- Read each question carefully, so that you know exactly what you have to do. If it's complicated, underline anything important and make sure that you do exactly as asked. If you have to give an answer in pounds, then pence will not do. If you are asked to state your units, you will lose marks if you write, for instance, 32 and not 32 cm.

- Always show your working. If the question asks for it, you will lose marks if you don't. Also, you may pick up some marks for your working, even if your final answer is wrong.

- Be careful when showing your working. If you are finding the area of a right-angled triangle, your calculation may be:

$(6 \times 4) \div 2 = 12$ cm^2, or

$6 \times 4 = 24$ cm^2

$24 \div 2 = 12$ cm^2

but not:

$6 \times 4 = 24 \div 2 = 12$ cm^2

6×4 does not equal $24 \div 2$ and you may lose marks if you say that it does.

- If you can't do something, leave it and come back to it later. Hopefully, the light will have dawned by then.

- If you finish early, check through everything very carefully, and try to fill in any gaps.

- Try to write something, even if you're not sure about it. You can't get any marks for an empty space, but you may pick up something even if you can't quite get the whole answer.

- Exams are important, but they aren't everything. Doing well in these tests will boost your confidence, but if they're a disaster, it's not the end of the world. They may be the first public exams that you have ever sat, so use the experience to help you to prepare for the next stage.

Good luck!

TEST PAPER 1

Mental arithmetic test

If possible, ask someone else to read this test aloud for you.

Section A

You have 5 seconds to answer each of these questions.

1   Write in figures the number that is nine more than one thousand.
2   How many millimetres are there in seven centimetres?
3   What is four multiplied by five multiplied by eight?
4   Multiply six point three by one thousand.
5   Simplify the expression $2t^2 + 5t^2$ as much as possible.
6   The probability of a bus being late is 0.75. What is the probability that it is on time?
7   Write the number 24.962 correct to one decimal place.
8   Subtract one hundred and seventy-four from two hundred and seventy-three.
9   Add together three hundred and fifty two and two hundred and forty seven.
10 Simplify the expression a times a^2 as much as possible.

Section B

You have 10 seconds to answer each of these questions.

11 I face west, then turn through 90° – clockwise, which way will I be facing? Circle the correct direction.
12 What is the value of the expression $3(c - 4)$ when $c = 10$?
13 What is the area of a triangle with base 6 cm and height 5 cm?
14 What is two hundred and fifty minus seventy-one?
15 What is ten per cent of thirty-nine pounds?
16 Seventy-four per cent of the members of a club are under twenty-five years old. What percentage are over twenty-five years?
17 By how many degrees must the temperature rise from negative two degrees to reach three degrees?
18 Robert is n years old. His sister is four years younger. Write an expression for her age.
19 Taking π as 3, what is the approximate area of a circle with a diameter of 20 metres?
20 Fifty per cent of a number is 17. What is the number?

Section C

You have 15 seconds to answer each of these questions.

21 Add the square root of twenty-five to the square root of sixteen.
22 In the diagram, rhombus A is rotated through 180°. Draw its image on rhombus B.
23 In a group of thirty boys and girls, the ratio of boys to girls is two to one. How many boys are there?
24 A square has an area of 49 cm². What is its perimeter?
25 Find the mean of the numbers 3, 8, 9, 12 and 23.
26 How much change would you get from £20.00 if you bought six books, each costing £2.99?
27 A train left the station at seven fifteen in the morning. The journey took one hour fifty minutes. What time did the train arrive?
28 The price of a shirt costing £40.00 is reduced in a sale by 15%. What is the new price?
29 Write an approximate answer for 59.8 ÷ 18.9.
30 The area of a square is 25 cm². If the length of the sides is doubled, what is the new area?

Mental arithmetic test

Response sheet

Section A	
1	
2	mm
3	
4	
5 $2t^2 + 5t^2$	
6	
7 24.962	to 1 d.p.
8 174 273	
9 352 247	
10 $a \times a^2$	

17
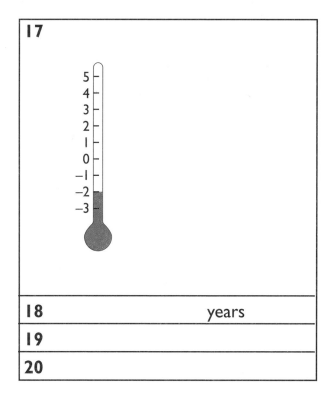

18	years
19	
20	

Section B
11 N E S W
12 $3(c - 4)$
13 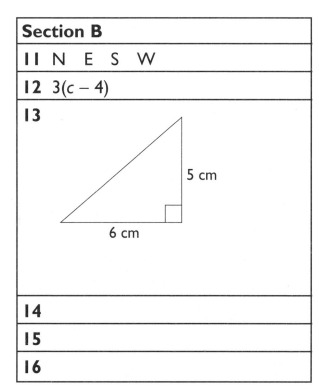
14
15
16

Section C
21
22 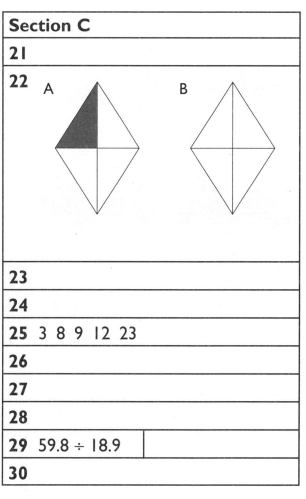
23
24
25 3 8 9 12 23
26
27
28
29 $59.8 \div 18.9$
30

TEST PAPER 2

Do not use a calculator for this paper.

Level 5

1   Here is a ready reckoner.   1 can costs 55p

                                    2 cans cost £1.10

                                    3 cans cost £1.65

                                    4 cans cost £2.20

                                    5 cans cost £2.75

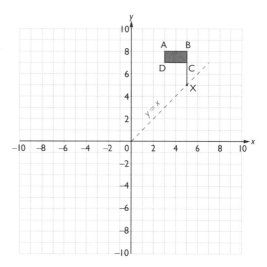

   Use it to help you to work out the cost of:

   a   6 cans _____   **b**   9 cans _____   **c**   10 cans _____

   d   20 cans _____   **e**   100 cans _____

2   When the flag is reflected in $y = x$:

   a   the coordinates of A′ are (___ , ___).

   b   the coordinates of D′ are (___ , ___)

   c   the point ___ does not move.

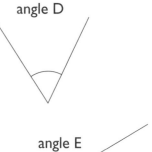

3   Which of these angles measures 60°?

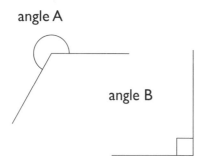

   Angle_____

4 Two children are playing a game. Each has seven cards.

Gail's are shown below.

They take turns to pick an instruction card. The instructions on Gail's cards were:

1 Make the smallest number that you can by adding the values on two cards together.

2 Score one point for every multiple of 5 that you hold.

3 Score two points for every integer that you hold.

4 Double the value of your highest card and add it to the value of your lowest card.

Fill in Gail's score sheet and find her total for the round.

✎ _____

	Score
Instruction 1	_____
Instruction 2	_____
Instruction 3	_____
Instruction 4	_____

5 Jamie is *n* years old.

His brother is 2 years older than he is.

His sister is 3 years younger than he is.

His mother is 5 times as old as he is.

Choose one of the following expressions to complete each sentence.

$n + 2$ $\quad 2n \quad$ n^2 $\quad n - 3 \quad$ $n + 5$ $\quad n + 3 \quad$ $3n$ $\quad 5n \quad$ $n - 2$ $\quad n$

✎ Jamie's brother is _____ years old.

✎ Jamie's sister is _____ years old.

✎ Jamie's mother is _____ years old.

6 16 people went out to a restaurant. They each decided to have the set meal costing £18.50.

a Work out the total bill.

✎ _____

b The restaurant adds 10% to the bill as a service charge. What should the bill be with the service charge included?

✎ _____

7 A bag has 20 cubes in it. Five of them are not red. Which values below show the probability of choosing a red cube? Underline the correct values.

75% $\frac{1}{4}$ 0.25   0.75   50% $\frac{3}{4}$ 25% $\frac{1}{2}$

Levels 5 and 6

8 a Vicky buys some trainers as advertised at a discount store. Work out the VAT at $17\frac{1}{2}$%.

_____

b How much does she pay for the trainers?

_____

c Later she visits a local shop and sees some shoes she likes just as much, that are reduced in a sale. Would she have better off buying them in the local shop? You must show enough working to support your answer.

_____

_____

_____

9 Solve the following equations.

a $x + 12 = 20$

  $x =$ _____

b $3w = 24$

  $w =$ _____

c $5t - 4 = 3t + 12$

  $t =$ _____

d $2(c + 3) = 20$

  $c =$ _____

10

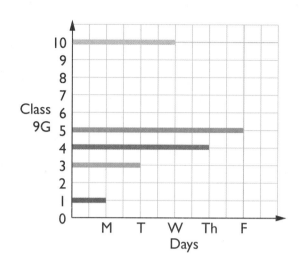
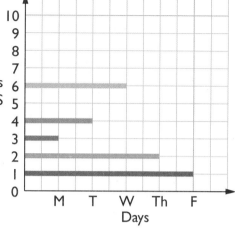

The graphs show the absences from school of a class over a school week in February.

a How many pupils were absent from class 9G on Tuesday?

_____

b How many pupils were absent from class 9S on Monday?

_____

c There was a school trip to the theatre which involved some pupils from both classes. On which day do you think it was?

_____

d How many more pupils were absent from 9G on Friday than were absent from 9S on Friday?

_____

e What additional information do you need before deciding which class had the higher percentage attendance that week?

_____

11 The formula for a sequence is $4n + 1$.

a Write down the first three numbers in the sequence.

_____

b Is the number 81 in the sequence? Give a reason for your answer.

_____

c Is the number 135 in the sequence? Show your working.

_____

12 a A sweet is taken from bag A. What is the probability that it is a caramel? Write your answer as a fraction in its lowest terms.

A   B

_____

b A sweet is taken from bag B. What is the probability that it is not a toffee? Write your answer as a fraction in its lowest terms.

_____

c The sweets are returned to the bags and a toffee from bag A is put into bag B. What is the probability of picking a caramel from bag A? Write this as a fraction in its lowest terms.

_____

d All the sweets are now tipped out of the bags. Richard shares them with his brother in the ratio 3 : 1. How many does he keep?

_____

13 a The diagram shows three nets for a cube.

   1   2   3

 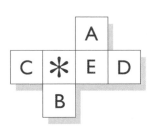 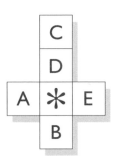

The starred face is always on the bottom.

Which face would be directly over the starred face in each cube?

  i   Face _____ is over the starred face.

  ii   Face _____ is over the starred face.

  iii   Face _____ is over the starred face.

14 In a class of 30 pupils, $\frac{2}{5}$ have brown eyes, the rest have blue eyes.

Three are left-handed. 6 walk to school. $\frac{1}{3}$ have a pet.

  a   What proportion are left-handed?

_____

b How many do not have brown eyes?

✎ _____

c How many have a pet?

✎ _____

d What fraction do not walk to school?

✎ _____

15 Paula sat five tests.

The mean of her results was 12.   The mode of her results was 10.

The range of her results was 5.   Her best result was 15.

Two and only two of her scores were consecutive numbers.

What were her results?

✎ _____

Levels 5–7

16 **a** Two integers multiplied together make –24, but added together make 2.

✎ The numbers are _____ and _____ .

b Two numbers multiplied together make –21 but added together make –4.

✎ The numbers are _____ and _____ .

c Two numbers multiplied together make 12 but added together make –8.

✎ The numbers are _____ and _____ .

d One square root of 100 is 10.

The other square root of 100 is _____ .

17 Write your answers as simply as possible without brackets.

✎ **a** The area of this rectangle is _____ cm^2.

The perimeter of this rectangle is _____ cm.

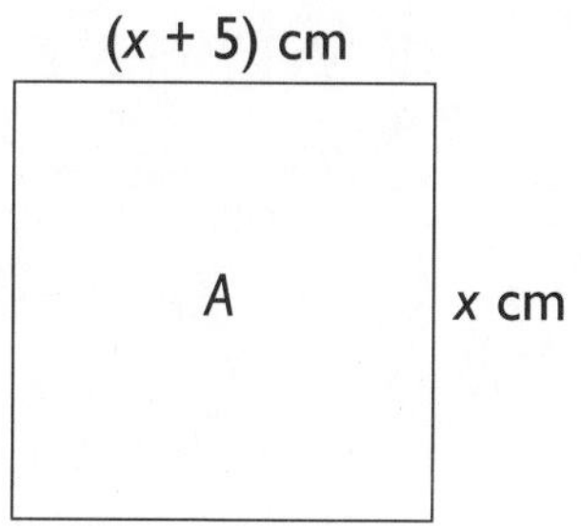

b The area of a square is 81 cm^2. What is its

perimeter? State your units.

✎

$(x + 5)$ cm

A x cm

_____

c The perimeter of a square is 20 cm. What is its area? State your units.

✎ _____

18 Research on children's learning included tests on their response times when completing certain tasks. The results have been recorded on this scatter graph.

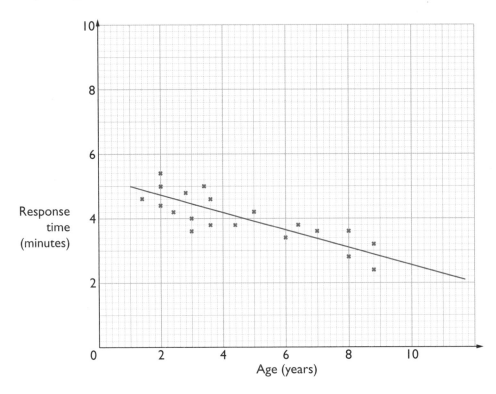

a What does the relationship between age and response time seem to be?

✎ _____

b Draw a line on your graph to estimate the time a five-year-old child might take to complete the task.

✎ _____

c Why might you not be able to extend the graph to include older people?

✎ _____

d Why, unlike many graphs, could you not extend this line indefinitely?

✎ _____

19 Simon is designing a poster to advertise a charity concert. He wants the heading to take up $\frac{1}{5}$ of the space and the information about prices to take up $\frac{1}{4}$ of the space. He wants to fill the remaining space with a coloured logo and the artists' names, in the ratio 6 : 5.

a What fraction of the space can he use for the logo and the names?

✎ _____

b What fraction of the original space will be taken up by the logo? Write your answer in its lowest terms.

✎ _____

20 The sketch shows a garden. The shaded area represents the lawn, and there is a path round it, with measurements as shown. Find the area of the path. Show your working, and remember to state the units used.

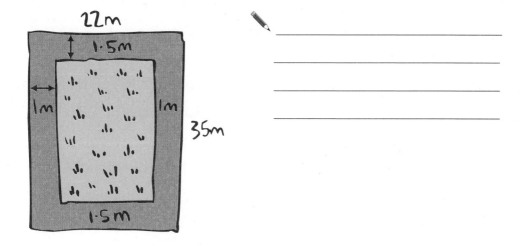

‎ _____

_____

_____

_____

21 Solve the following simultaneous equations. Do not use trial and improvement.

$4x + 3y = 44$

$5x + 2y = 41$

‎ _____

_____

_____

_____

22 ABDEG is a regular pentagon.
AB and AG are extended
to make triangle ACF as shown

a Find the size of these angles.

‎ $w =$ _____   ‎ $x =$ _____

‎ $y =$ _____   ‎ $z =$ _____

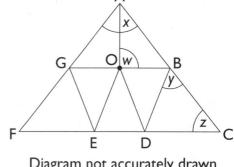

Diagram not accurately drawn

b Does BD = BC? Give a reason for your answer.
The diagram is not drawn accurately so you must answer the questions by calculation and not measurement. Show your working.

‎ _____

You may use a calculator to help you with any question on this paper.

Level 5

1 A group of 17 people decided to share a bill for a meal equally. The bill was £211.75. How much should each pay, to the nearest penny?

_____

2 Marian is going on holiday. She has decided to save $12\frac{1}{2}$% of any money she has towards it, rounding any amount to the nearest 50p. For her birthday she had £75.50 altogether. How much does she plan to save?

_____

3 Niall is trying to work out the distance between Bathfield and Little Bingham, for his French exchange visitor. At last he remembers that there are roughly 8 kilometres in 5 miles. How far, in kilometres, is it from Bathfield to Little Bingham?

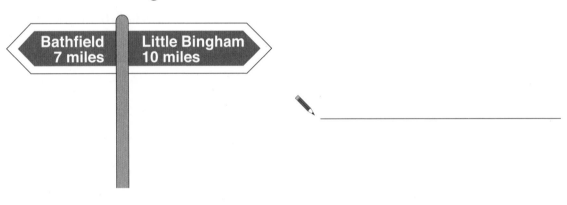

_____

4 Sean has two spare tickets for a concert. Andrea, Keith, Ahmed, Sunita and Louise want to go. Keith and Louise have broken up and won't go together. Write the possible pairs that could go. One has been done for you.

Ahmed and Andrea

_____

5 Triangle A is rotated 90° anticlockwise around O. Draw the new position of triangle A. You may use tracing paper to help you.

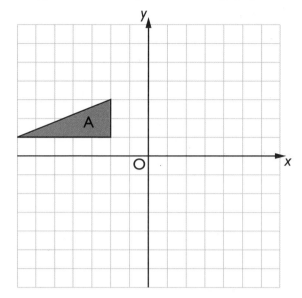

6 The twins Lee and Yvette are redecorating their bedrooms. They have bought some small tester pots of paint to try out various colours.

Yvette likes orange and mixes three tins of red and one of yellow.

a What is the ratio of her mixture, red : yellow?

_____

What fraction of her mixture is red paint and what fraction is yellow?

_____

Lee prefers green. He wants to use twice as much yellow as blue.

b If he use whole tins at a time, what is the minimum number of tins he must mix together?

_____

What fraction will he have of each colour?

_____

TEST PAPER 3

Levels 5–6

7 a A circle has a diameter of 15 cm. What is its area? Show your working and give your answer to 1 d.p.

_____

b Another circle has a circumference of 25 cm. What is its radius, correct to 1 d.p?

_____

8 A rectangle has width w and its length is 3 cm greater.

The area of the rectangle is 75.25 cm².

Use trial and improvement to find w, correct to 1 d.p.

w	$w + 3$	$w(w + 3)$	Comment
7	10	70	too small
8	11	88	too big

9 Work out the values of l and m.

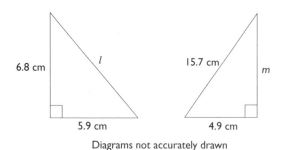

6.8 cm l 15.7 cm m

5.9 cm   4.9 cm

Diagrams not accurately drawn

_____

10 The table below shows the percentage of candidates who opted to take Business Studies as an option.

2000	15.4%
2001	17.3%

From the information supplied, tick the correct statement.

❑   In 2000 fewer students chose to take Business Studies than in 2001.

❑   In 2001, more students chose to take Business Studies than in 2000.

❑   There is not enough information to tell whether more or fewer students chose Business Studies in either year.

11 Jo and Sue are playing ten games in a competition.

So far Jo has played five games. Her average score is 3.4.

Sue has played seven games and her total score is fourteen.

a Who has the better record?

_____

Sue wants to double her average score.

b What does she need to score in total in the remaining games?

_____

Jo wants to improve her average to five. She loses the next two games, so scores no points.

c How many does she need to average on her remaining games to achieve her target?

_____

12 Harry has been appointed head gardener at a stately home and is replanning some of the garden. He needs to replace some of the trees, rose bushes and shrubs. He also needs to buy fertiliser and replace some garden tools. He has been given a budget and intends to allocate the money as follows.

Trees   35%

Rose bushes   27%

Shrubs   18%

Fertiliser   12%

Tools   8%

a The estate manager displays this information on a pie chart.

What angle does he draw for each sector? Answer to the nearest degree.

Trees _____   Rose bushes _____   Shrubs _____

Fertiliser _____   Tools _____

b He has £50 000 to spend. How much should he spend on each category?

_____

13 a Work out a rough answer for this problem.

$$\frac{39.84 \times 24.9}{212.1 - 111.8}$$

_____

b Use your calculator to work out the correct answer.

Write down all the digits on your calculator display.

_____

14 Simplify the following expressions.

a $4f + 5g - 7f + 2g$

_____

b $-2f - (-6f)$

_____

c $3d^2 + 5d - d^2 + 1$

_____

Levels 5–7

15 ABCD is a parallelogram with vertical height BX.

AB = 6.2 cm

AD = 7.3 cm

DX = 2.4 cm

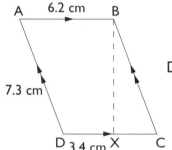

Diagram not to scale

a Write down the length of CX.

_____

b Find the length BX and use it to find the area of the parallelogram.
Give your answer correct to 2 s.f.

_____

16 In the imperial measurement system:

3 feet = 1 yard

220 yards = 1 furlong

8 furlongs = 1 mile

a The Derby horse race is run over $1\frac{1}{2}$ miles. How many feet is that?

_____

_____

b How many km are approximately equal to $1\frac{1}{2}$ miles?

_____

17 Point A is at (2, 4).

It comes in the part of the graph where $y > x$, because $4 > 2$, and where $y < 6$ and $x < 6$.

(2, 4) is also in the part of the graph where $y < 8 - x$, because $4 < 8 - 2$.

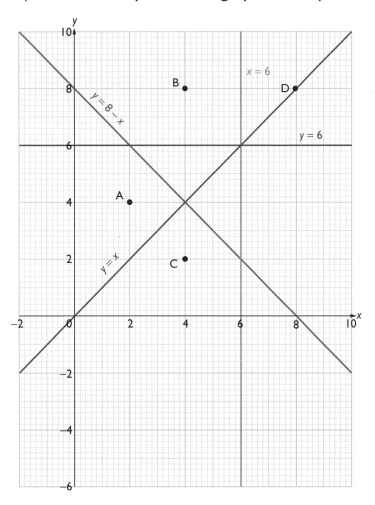

Now fill in the spaces using the signs:

less than <   equal to =   greater than >

a Point A comes in the part of the graph where y _____ x and y _____ $8 - x$.

b Point B comes in the part of the graph where y _____ $8 - x$ and x _____ 6.

c Point C comes in the part of the graph where y _____ x and y _____ 6.

d Point D comes in the part of the graph where y _____ x.

18 A cylinder with base radius 15 cm and height 50 cm is filled with liquid.

   a What is the area of the base? Give your answer correct to 2 d.p.

   b How much liquid is in the cylinder? Give your answer in litres, to the nearest litre.

19 A bag contains red cubes and blue cubes in the ratio 5 : 3.

   a A cube is chosen at random. What is the probability that it is not red?

   b A red cube is removed from the bag. What is the smallest number of red cubes that could still be in the bag?

   c Originally, 12 blue cubes were placed in the bag. How many red cubed were there?

20 In the diagram, FC and XY are lines of symmetry.

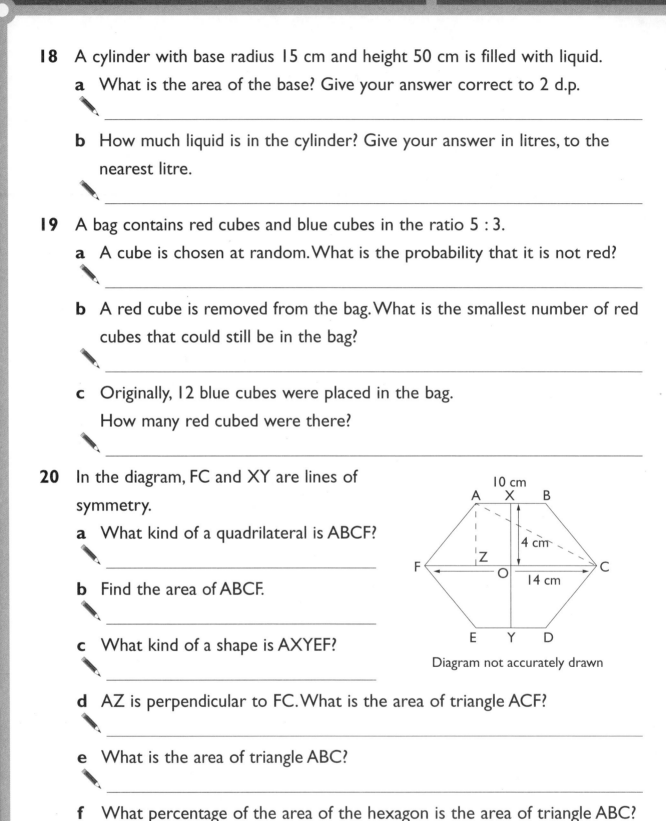

Diagram not accurately drawn

   a What kind of a quadrilateral is ABCF?

   b Find the area of ABCF.

   c What kind of a shape is AXYEF?

   d AZ is perpendicular to FC. What is the area of triangle ACF?

   e What is the area of triangle ABC?

   f What percentage of the area of the hexagon is the area of triangle ABC?

21 The L-shape on the grid is transformed by an enlargement, scale factor $\frac{1}{2}$, centred at $(0, 0)$.

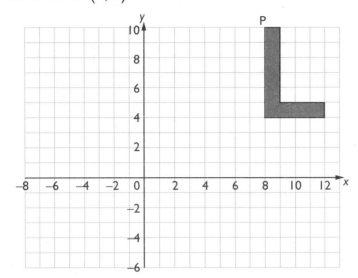

a What are the coordinates of the image P′ under this enlargement?

_____

b The point P′ is then reflected in the y-axis. What are the coordinates of its image?

_____

c Complete the following sentence.

The point can be returned to its original position by moving it left/right _____ and up/down _____ .

89

ANSWERS

Answers to exercises

Number and algebra

Unit 1   Rounding

Exercise 1 (page 8)
1   **a** 0.9 **b** 4.3 **c** 0.5 **d** 9.0 **e** 8.0
2   **a** 2000 **b** 300 **c** 5000
3   **a** 0.9 **b** 4 **c** 0.5 **d** 9 **e** 8

Exercise 2 (page 9)
1   350 cm shortest, 450 cm longest
2   69.5 shortest and 70.5 cm longest.
3   59 500 smallest and 60 500 greatest

Unit 2   Problems

Exercise 1 (page 10)
1   $30 \times 5 = 150$, $35 + 15 = 50$,
    $150 \div 50 = 3$
2   $(29.8 \times 5.1) \div (35.2 + 15.4) = 3$ to 1 s.f.

Exercise 2 (page 11)
1   $\frac{1}{4}$ of $40 = 40 \div 4 = 10$
    Natalie kept 10 pieces.
    She gave Colin 30 pieces.
    Colin kept $\frac{2}{5}$ of $30 = 30 \div 5 \times 2 = 12$.
    He gave Anna $30 - 12 = 18$ pieces.
    Anna ate $\frac{1}{2}$ of $18 = 18 \div 2 = 9$.
    She gave Tim 9 pieces.
    Tim gave Natalie $9 - 5 = 4$ pieces.
    Natalie had $10 + 4 = 14$ pieces
2   $15\% + 45\% = 60\%$ $100\% - 60\% = 40\%$
    40% came by car

Unit 3 Multiplying and dividing fractions and decimals

Exercise 1 (page 12)
1   $12 \times \frac{3}{4}$ smaller than 12, bigger than $\frac{3}{4}$.
2   $\frac{3}{5} \times 17$ smaller than 17, bigger than $\frac{3}{5}$.
3   $\frac{1}{2} \times \frac{3}{4}$ is smaller than 1.

Exercise 2 (page 13)
1   $4 \div 0.5$ is bigger than 4.
2   1.2 divided by 3 is smaller than 3.
3   $0.8 \div 0.2$ is bigger than 0.8.

Unit 4 Proportion and ratio

Exercise 1 (page 14)
1   **a** £14.25 **b** £142.50 **c** 18
2   **a** 2 eggs
    b $1\frac{1}{3}$ eggs. You would find it hard to weigh out a third
    of an egg, so choose one or two.
    c 1 egg **d** 2 or 3 ($2\frac{2}{3}$ eggs)

Exercise 2 (page 15)
1   **a** 2 : 1 **b** 30 m² **c** 90 m²
    d 3 : 2 = 5 parts altogether.
    $90 \div 5 = 18$, vegetables: $3 \times 18 = 54$ m²,
    flowers $2 \times 18 = 36$ m²

Unit 5 Simplifying algebra

Exercise 1 (page 18)
1   $3a + 7b$ **2** $9f - 3g$ **3** $4m - 4m^2$

Exercise 2 (page 18)
1   **a** $11x + 5g$ **b** $7y^2 + 3y - 2xy$
2   **a** $15h + 6j - 12c^2$
    b $5d - 10 - 3d - 6 = 2d - 16$

Exercise 3 (page 19)
1   $(x + 6)(x + 3) = x^2 + 3x + 6x + 18$
    $= x^2 + 9x + 18$
2   $(b + 2)(b - 4) = b^2 - 4b + 2b - 8$
    $= b^2 - 2b - 8$
3   $(p - 3)(p + 2) = p^2 + 2p - 3p - 6$
    $= p^2 - p - 6$ $(p = 1p)$

4   $(d - 4)(d - 1) = d^2 - d - 4d + 4$
    $= d^2 - 5d + 4$

Exercise 4 (page 19)
1   $(x - 3)(x - 8) = x^2 - 8x - 3x + 24$
    $= x^2 - 11x + 24$
2   $(e + 2)(e - 7) = e^2 - 7e + 2e - 14$
    $= e^2 - 5e - 14$
3   $(a - 4)(a + 5) = a^2 + 5a - 4a - 20$
    $= a^2 + a - 20$
4   $(y + 10)(y + 3) = y^2 + 3y + 10y + 30$
    $= y^2 + 13y + 30$

Unit 6 Simultaneous equations

Exercise 1 (page 20)
1   $x = 2, y = 8$ **2** $x = 10, y = 3$
3   $x = 12, y = 5$

Exercise 2 (page 21)
1   $x = 3, y = 10$ **2** $x = 1, y = 5$

Exercise 3 (page 22)
1   $x = 6, y = 5$ **2** $x = 10, y = 4$

Exercise 4 (page 23)
1   $x = 2, y = 3$ **2** $x = 1, y = 5$
3   $x = 7, y = 2$

Exercise 5 (page 24)
1   $x = 2, y = 4$ **2** $x = 4, y = 8$
3   $x = 1, y = 5$

Exercise 6 (page 25)

$y = x + 3$					
x	−2	−1	0	1	2
y	1	2	3	4	5

$y = 2x + 4$					
x	−2	−1	0	1	2
y	0	2	4	6	8

$x = -1, y = 2$

Unit 7 Graphs, lines, equations

Exercise 1 (page 26)
1   B: $y = x$ **2** A: $x = 3$ **3** D: $y = \frac{1}{2}x + 4$.
4   C: $y = -4$. **5** E: $y = \frac{1}{2}x - 4$

Exercise 2 (page 27)
1   **a** No, $3 \times 5 + 1$ does not equal 17.
    b Yes, $2 \times 2 + 9 = 13$
2   $11 = 8b - 5$, $16 = 8b$, $b = 2$
    The equation is $y = 2x - 5$.

Unit 8 Inequalities

Exercise 1 (page 28)
1   $5 < 6$ **2** $-2 > -3$ **3** $8 > 2$ **4** $-10 < -4$

Exercise 2 (page 28)
1   **a** $s < 4$ **b** $5s \geqslant 10, s \geqslant 2$ **c** $d > 8$
2   **a** 4 **b** 4, 5

Unit 9 Sequences

Exercise 1 (page 29)
1   **a** $-1, 1, 3$
2   $2n - 3 = 502$, $2n = 505$, $n = 252.5$, no, 502 isn't a term.
3   35 and 59
4   **a** 2, 8, 18, 32
    b The differences are 6, 10, 14; increasing by 4.

Shape, space and measures

Unit 10 Pythagoras' theorem

Exercise 1 (page 32)
1   PR = 8.2 cm to 1 d.p. **2** PR = 9.9 cm to 1 d.p.

Exercise 2 (page 33)
1   $25 + 144 = 169$, $\sqrt{100} = 13$
    The hypotenuse is 13 cm long.
2   **a** The hypotenuse would be 20 cm
    b The triangle has been enlarged by a scale factor of 4.

Exercise 3 (page 34)
1 The third side is 20.8 cm to 1 d.p.
2 The third side cannot be longer than the hypotenuse.
   (Peter added the squares instead of subtracting them.)
   The third side is 18.8 cm

Exercise 4 (page 35)
1 20.7 cm **2 a** 9 cm **b** 18 cm

Unit 11 Enlargements

Exercise 1 (page 36)
1 Centre (0, 0) sometimes called the origin.
   Scale factor = 4

Exercise 2 (page 37)
1

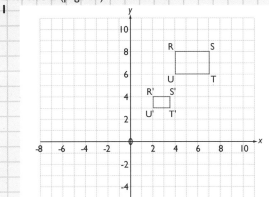

   The coordinates of S′ are (3.5, 4).
2 Scale factor = $\frac{1}{4}$ **3** Scale factor = 2

Unit 12 Constructions and loci

Exercise 1 (page 38)
1 The perpendicular bisector of RS.
2 A circle centred at H with radius 7 cm.
3 A line which bisects angle QRS.

Exercise 2 (page 39)
1

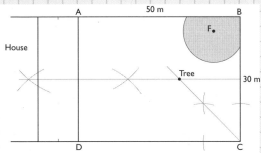

Unit 13 Distance, speed and time

Exercise 1 (page 40)

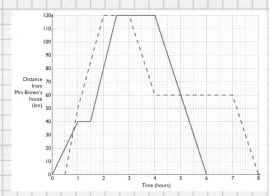

Exercise 2 (page 41)
1 300 km **2** 2.5 hours = 2 hours 30 minutes
3 340 ÷ 3.25 = 104.615 = 105 km/h to 3 s.f.

Unit 14 Area and perimeter

Exercise 1 (page 42)
1 The area of trapezium D is 91 cm^2.
2 The area of trapezium E is 81 cm^2.
3 The area of trapezium F is 85.68 cm^2.

Exercise 2 (page 43)
1 77 cm^2 **2** 46.17 cm^2 **3** 357 cm^2

Exercise 3 (page 44)
1 **a** s^2 cm^2 **b** $4s$ cm **c** either $\frac{1}{2}s^2$ or $\frac{s^2}{2}$ cm^2
2 **a** t cm **b** $4v$ cm

Exercise 4 (page 45)
1 $4n$ cm^2 **2** $2n + 16$ cm
3 **a** $3n$ and 4 cm **b** $6n + 8$ cm **c** $12n$ cm^2

Unit 15 Circles

Exercise 1 (page 46)
1 area = 564 cm^2, circumference = 84 cm
2 40 ÷ π = 12.7 cm
3 100 ÷ π = 31.83, 31.83 ÷ 2 = 15.9 cm
4 **a** 10 cm **b** 5 cm, 78.5 cm^2 **c** 21.5%
5 **a** 15 cm **b** 353 cm^2

Exercise 2 (page 47)
1 circumference = 4.7 m, distance = 4.7 × 20 = 94.2 m
2 circumference = 204 cm = 2.04 m
   number of turns = 1000 ÷ 2.04 = 489 turns
3 The length is the same as the circumference of the tin.
   32.986… cm   33.0 cm to 3 s.f.
4 circumference = 1 m = 100 cm
   diameter = 31.8 cm to 1 d.p.

Unit 16 Volume

Exercise 1 (page 48)
1 1080 **2 a** 421.875 cm^3 **b** 422 cm^3

Exercise 2 (page 49)
1 577.3 cm^3
2 **a** volume = 50 265.48 cm^3 = 50.265 litres
   b number of glasses = 50.265 ÷ 0.2 = 251 glasses

Exercise 3 (page 50)
1 765 cm^3 **2** 1400 cm^3

Exercise 4 (page 51)
1 8 × 6 × 2 = 96
2 length × width = 200
   volume = length × width × height
   1200 = 20 × 10 × ?
   1200 = 200 × ?
   height = 1200 ÷ 200 = 6 cm

Data handling

Unit 17 Questions and answers

Exercise 1 (page 54)
There is more than one answer, but these are possibilities.
1 People would use a new bus service on this route.
2 People would use this coach service to visit the cinema.

Exercise 2 (page 55)
1

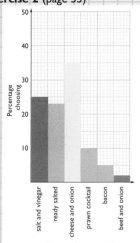

2

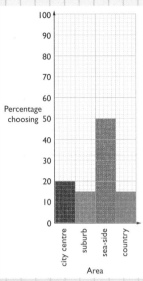

3 $360° = 100\%$
city centre $20\% = 72°$ suburb $15\% = 54°$
seaside $50\% = 180°$ countryside $15\% = 54°$

Unit 18 Scatter graphs

Exercise 1 (page 56)
1 C   **2** Positive correlation.
3 A   **4** B

Exercise 2 (page 57)
1 Negative correlation   **2** About 54 minutes
3 The student who trained for 16 minutes and completed
   the task in 15 minutes

Unit 19 Averages and range

Exercise 1 (page 58)
1 Total = 19, mean = $19 \div 5 = 3.8$, median = 3.9, mode =
   2.7, range = $5.6 - 2.7 = 2.9$
2 Total = $6x + 3 + 4x + 5 = 10x + 8$
   There are two cards, so the mean is
   $(10x + 8) \div 2 = 5x + 4$

Exercise 2 (page 59)
1 6   **2** 11   **3** 10

Exercise 3 (page 60)
1 £136.00   **2** Mean = £3.89
3 Mode = £4.00 and £5.00

Exercise 4 (page 61)
1

Marks gained	Number of students	Mid-interval value
0–5	3	2.5
6–10	14	8
11–15	10	13
16–20	3	18

2 Modal group is 6–10
3 $2.3 \times 2.5 + 14 \times 8 + 10 \times 13 + 3 \times 18$
   $= 303.5$
   mean = $303.5 \div 30 = 10.1 = 10$ marks

Unit 20 Frequency polygons
Exercise 1 (page 62)

a

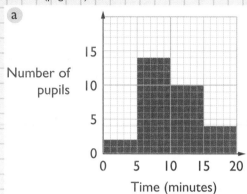

b

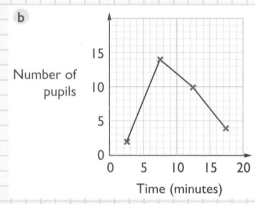

Exercise 2 (page 63)
1 750g to 1 kg
2 The modal group would still be 750 g to 1 kg as it
   would still have most members.

Unit 21 Probability

Exercise 1 (page 64)
1 certain   **2** impossible
3 Likely (It is not certain, since there may be female
   members of staff or you may meet a pupil's
   female relative.)
4 There is the same number, i.e. 20 of each.

Exercise 2 (page 65)
1 4 crosses and 1 star
2 **a** all stars   **b** 2 crosses and 3 stars

Exercise 3 (page 66)
1 probability of a loss = 0.2, $0.2 \times 20 = 4$
2 $\frac{6000}{30000} = \frac{1}{5}$ or 0.2   **3** $0.2 \times 45\,000 = 9000$

Exercise 4 (page 67)
1 **a**

×	2	2	4	7
1	2	2	4	7
2	4	4	8	14
2	4	4	8	14
5	10	10	20	35

   b $\frac{5}{16}$ **c** $\frac{1}{4}$ **d** 0

2 $\frac{5}{16}$ of 64 = 20
3 Andrew is right. The area of each spinner where 2 can
   be scored is $\frac{1}{2}$ for each.
4 It seems unlikely, but she needs to spin the spinners
   more times to be sure.

Answers to tests

Test paper 1 (page 72)
1 1009   **2** 70 mm   **3** 160
4 6300   **5** $7t^2$ **6** 0.25   **7** 25.0
8 99   **9** 599   **10** a^3

11 north **12** 18 **13** 15 cm²
14 179 **15** £3.90 **16** 26%
17 5 degree° **18** $n - 4$
19 300 m² (radius = 10 m, $3 \times 10^2 = 300$) **20** 34
21 9
22

23 20 boys
24 Each side is 7 cm so the perimeter is 28 cm.
25 11 **26** £2.06 **27** 9.05 a.m. **28** £34.00
29 This is approximately $60 \div 20 = 3$
30 100 cm² (The original sides are 5 cm, so the new lengths are 10 cm. $10^2 = 100$)

Test Paper 2 (page 74)

1 **a** £3.30 **b** £4.95 **c** £5.50 **d** £11.00 **e** £55.00
2 **a** (8, 3) **b** (7, 3) **c** X
3 D
4

	Score
Instruction 1	−10
Instruction 2	1
Instruction 3	12
Instruction 4	$16 - 7 = 9$
Total = $22 - 10 = 12$	

5 Jamie's brother is $n + 2$ years old.
Jamie's sister is $n - 3$ years old.
Jamie's mother is $5n$ years old.
6 **a** £296.00 **b** £325.60
7 75%, 0.75, $\frac{3}{4}$
8 **a** £5.25 **b** £30.00 + £5.25 = £35.25
   c 15% of £40.00 = £6.00
   The shoes in the local shop cost £34.00, so she would have saved money if she had bought them.
9 **a** $x = 8$ **b** $w = 8$ **c** $t = 8$ **d** $c = 7$
10 **a** 3 **b** 3
   c Wednesday because that was the day on which the highest total absence was recorded.
   d 4
   e How many pupils there were altogether in each class
11 **a** 5, 9, 13
   b Yes. $4n + 1 = 81, 4n = 80, n = 20$
   c No. $4n + 1 = 135, 4n = 134, n = 33\frac{1}{2}$ n must be a whole number, so 135 is not in the sequence.
12 **a** $\frac{6}{16} = \frac{3}{8}$ **b** $\frac{10}{16} = \frac{5}{8}$ **c** $\frac{6}{15} = \frac{2}{5}$
   d $32 \div 4 = 8$ Richard keeps $8 \times 3 = 24$
13 **a** i B ii D iii C
14 **a** $\frac{1}{10}$ **b** 18 pupils **c** 10 **d** $\frac{4}{5}$
15 10, 10, 12, 13, 15
16 **a** 6 and −4 **b** −7 and 3 **c** −6 and −2 **d** −10
17 **a** $x(x + 5) = x^2 + 5x, 4x + 10$
   b 36 cm **c** 25 cm²
18 **a** The older the child, the less time takes. Negative correlation.
   b Almost 4 minutes
   c It is possible that people do not go on improving, the older they get.
   d You would have subjects with negative ages and older people would respond in a negative amount of time.
19 **a** $\frac{11}{20}$ **b** $\frac{3}{10}$
20 Area of path = 770 m² − 640 m² = 130 m²
21 $x = 5, y = 8$

22 **a** $w = 360° \div 5 = 72°$
   b $x = 108°$ ($\angle BAO = \frac{1}{2}(180 - 72) = 54°$ but $x = 2 \times \angle BAO = 108°$)
   c $y = 72°$ ($\angle ABD = \angle BAG = 108°$, $y = 180° - 108° = 72°$ as angles on a straight line add up to 180°)
   d $z = 36°$ ($\triangle$ ACF is isosceles, $z = \frac{1}{2}(180° - 108°) = 36°$)
   e BD is not equal to DC because $y \neq z$.

Test Paper 3 (page 82)

1 £12.46 **2** £9.50
3 $\frac{8}{5}$ km, 27.2 km
4 Ahmed and Andrea   Ahmed and Keith
   Ahmed and Sunita   Ahmed and Louise
   Keith and Andrea   Keith and Sunita
   Sunita and Andrea   Sunita and Louise
   Louise and Andrea
5

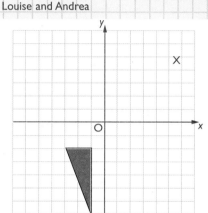

6 **a** 3 : 1; $\frac{3}{4}$ red, $\frac{1}{4}$ yellow **b** 3 tins; $\frac{2}{3}$ yellow, $\frac{1}{3}$ blue
7 **a** 176.7 cm² ($A = \pi r^2$)
   b 4.0 cm ($C = \pi d$ so $d = C \div \pi, r = \frac{1}{2}d$)
8 7.3 cm
9 $l = 9.0$ cm, $m = 14.9$ cm
10 There is not enough information. If there were fewer candidates, 17.3%, though a larger percentage than 15.4% might be a smaller actual number.
11 **a** Jo's average so far is higher than Sue's.
   b Sue needs a total of 40. Her total is 14, so she needs another 26.
   c For Jo to average 5, she needs a total of $10 \times 5 = 50$. She needs to score $50 - 17 = 33$. She has 3 games remaining, so needs to average 11 on each game to achieve her target.
12 **a** Trees 126°, rose bushes 97°, shrubs 65°, fertiliser 43°, tools 29°
   b Trees £17 500, rose bushes £13 500, shrubs £9000, fertiliser £6000, tools £4000
13 **a** 10 **b** 9.890 488 534 4
14 **a** $-3f + 7g$ **b** $4f$ **c** $2d^2 + 5d + 1$
15 **a** 2.8 cm **b** 42 cm²
16 **a** 7920 feet **b** 2.4 km
17 **a** Point A comes in the part of the graph where $y > x$ and $y < 8 - x$.
   b Point B comes in the part of the graph where $y > 8 - x$ and $x < 6$.
   c Point C comes in the part of the graph where $y < x$ and $y < 6$.
   d Point D comes in the part of the graph where $y = x$.
18 **a** 706.86 cm² **b** 35 litres
19 **a** $\frac{3}{8}$ **b** 4 **c** 20 red
20 **a** trapezium **b** 48 cm² **c** pentagon **d** 28 cm²
   e 20 cm² **f** 20.8%
21 **a** (4, 5) **b** (−4, 5)
   c The point can be returned to its original position by moving it right 12 and up 5.

angle	amount or turn where two (or more) lines meet
area	the flat space occupied by a shape, or inside it
axis of symmetry	mirror line
axis (plural axes)	the vertical or horizontal line on a graph; the line that divides a symmetrical shape into two exact mirror images
biased	event which is more likely to give one outcome than another (If all outcomes are equally likely, the event is **unbiased**.)
common denominator	a number into which two or more numbers will divide exactly.
commutative	an operation where the order does not matter (Multiplication is commutative because $3 \times 2 = 2 \times 3$.)
congruent	identical
consecutive	following without a gap
consecutive numbers	numbers that follow on in order, e.g. 1, 2, 3, …
cube	a 3D solid with square faces
cuboid	a 3D solid with rectangular faces
decagon	a ten-sided polygon
denominator	the bottom number in a fraction showing how many parts there are in the whole
digit	individual numeral in a number: 6 has one digit, 20 has two digits, as does 3.4
dividend	a number or quantity to be divided (In the example $6 \div 2$, six is the dividend.)
divisor	the number that is divided by (In the example $6 \div 2$, two is the divisor.)
edge	where two faces of a solid meet
equidistant	at the same distance from
equilateral	equal sided
evaluate	find the value
expression	two or more terms in a formula, e.g. $4n + 2$
exterior angle	the angle formed at a vertex (corner) outside a polygon if one side is extended
factor	a number that divides into another number or quantity exactly, e.g. 4 is a factor of 8
frequency	the number of times an event happens
frequency diagram	a diagram to show the frequency of an event, e.g. a bar chart
front elevation	the view of an object from the front
gradient	measure of steepness or slope
hexagon	a six-sided polygon
highest common factor	the largest number which will divide exactly into two or more numbers without giving a fractional answer or leaving a remainder
horizontal axis	the axis in a graph that goes across, usually the x-axis (The **horizon** is **horizontal**.)
hypotenuse	the longest side in a right-angled triangle, opposite the right angle
integer	whole number
interior angle	the angle inside the vertex (corner) of a polygon
intersect	cross (Lines that cross each other are intersecting lines.)
intersection	the point where two lines cross
inverse process	a process that 'undoes' the previous process (Addition and subtraction are inverse processes, and multiplication and division are inverse processes.)
isosceles triangle	a triangle with two sides the same and two angles the same
lowest common denominator	the smallest number into which two or more denominators will divide, used when adding or subtracting fractions
lowest common multiple	the smallest number into which two or more numbers will divide, used to find the lowest common denominator
mean	the sum of all the values in a set of data, divided by the number of values in the set
median	the middle value of a set of data arranged in order from left to right, smallest to largest
modal group	the range of values that occurs most often (has the highest frequency) in a set of grouped data, e.g. ages 5–9
mode	the most common value in a given set (the value with the highest frequency)
multiple	a number with two or more factors, a number formed by multiplying two other numbers, e.g. 12 is a multiple of 3, 20 is a multiple of 10

multiplier	scale factor
net	a hollow 3D shape opened up and laid flat
numeral	single figure in a number, like a letter in a word
numerator	the top number in a fraction showing how many of the equal parts of the whole are being considered
octagon	an eight-sided polygon
outcome	the result of an event in probability (Throwing a penny has two possible outcomes, head or tail.)
parallel	two (or more) lines that are always equidistant from each other (Spelling hint: The two letter ls in the word 'parallel' are parallel lines.)
parallelogram	a four-sided shape with one pair of opposite sides equal and parallel (In fact, both pairs are equal and parallel, but the proof will come in later years.)
pentagon	a five-sided polygon
perimeter	the distance all round a shape
perpendicular	meeting or intersecting at right angles (90°)
plan view	a view of an object looking down from above
polygon	a two-dimensional (2D), straight-sided shape with three or more sides
probability scale	a measure of probability, like a number line, from 0 to 1
product	the result of multiplying two numbers together
quadrant	a quarter of a graph grid (The x- and y-axes divide a graph into four quadrants.)
quadrilateral	a four-sided polygon
quotient	the result of dividing a number or amount by another number (In $6 \div 2 = 3$, the quotient is 3.)
random	by chance (A random sample is one in which all members of the group have equal chances of being chosen.)
range	the largest value minus the smallest value in a set of data
rhombus	a quadrilateral with all sides equal and opposite sides parallel (The diagonals cross at right angles.)
sample	group or people taken as being typical, to take part in a survey

scale factor	the number by which every length of a shape is multiplied in an enlargement.
scalene triangle	triangle in which each side is a different length and all angles are different
sequence of numbers	a list of numbers that form a pattern according to a given rule
side elevation	the view of an object from the side
similar	exactly the same shape but different sizes; one shape is an enlargement of the other, so all the corresponding angles are equal, the sides are in the same proportion (the scale factor)
simplify	collect together all the same variables in an expression or equation, e.g. $1 + 2t + 1 + 3t + 2 = 5t + 4$
sum	the total of two or more numbers added together
survey	research, find out people's opinions by asking questions
term	a number in a sequence (The first number is the first term, the next is the second term, and so on.)
trapezium	a quadrilateral with one pair of sides parallel but unequal
unbiased	an event in which all outcomes have an equal chance of occurring
variable	numbers that do not necessarily have a fixed value, but vary, usually represented by letters in algebra
vertex	corner (The plural is **vertices**.)
vertical	upright
vertical axis	the axis in a graph that goes up and down the page, at right angles o the horizontal axis, and usually called the y-axis
vertices	corners, plural of vertex

Symbols

$<$	means 'is less than'
$>$	means 'is greater than'
$\leqslant$	means 'is less than or equal to', or 'is not greater than'
$\geqslant$	means 'is greater than or equal to', or 'is not less than'

INDEX